NATURE'S
SILENT
MESSAGE

SCOTT STILLMAN

NATURE'S SILENT MESSAGE

WILD
SOUL
PRESS

Wild Soul Press
Boulder, Colorado

Design and layout: Andrea Costantine
Editors: Emma Murray, Alexandra O'Connell

Front Cover: Dirty Devil Wilderness (photo by Scott Stillman)
Back Cover: Black Ridge Canyons Wilderness
(photo by Scott Stillman)

Library of Congress Cataloging-in-Publication Data
Stillman, Scott
Nature's Silent Message / Scott Stillman
LCCN 2020903709

ISBN: 978-1-7323522-2-3

WILD
SOUL
PRESS

Contents

Preface

A new beginning...

It's been six months since the release of *Wilderness, The Gateway to the Soul*. Mixing passion with business is a tricky enterprise—Amazon, Facebook, editors, reviews—the whole thing an emotional rollercoaster of ups, downs, successes, and failures. Yet here we are with over 20,000 copies sold. Not bad I guess, for an indie book. Thanks for reading.

My heart and soul are in that book—fully exposed—open for anyone to criticize, love, or hate. At least it's the truth. Take it or leave it, the book is no lie. Now you know who I am.

Well, enough about the past.

Like any true romantic, I'm taking the money and running, away from the city lights and back to the real world—beyond the pavement.

What I crave—as always—is the next journey, the next passage, the next chapter. To walk out into the wilderness and see what comes—not what comes to mind—but what comes. There's a not-so-subtle difference. One requires much thought and deliberation—too much work. The other allows the pen to move freely and effortlessly—nature's way.

Nature speaks a silent message that can be heard when conditions are just right. You cannot hear it from the city. Believe me, I've tried.

Truth exists in wild places—where the air is clean, the water pure, the land free.

It's time to lose the baggage, put down the gadgets, take a long walk.

See you on the other side...

S. STILLMAN
Tucson, Arizona
March 2019

Why Go to the Wilderness?

To laugh at the stars,
To talk to the birds.
To understand the landscape
But use no words.
To forget about time
And remember who you are.
To feel God
Surrendering to a star.

NATURE'S
SILENT
MESSAGE

CHAPTER ONE

Death Hollow, Utah

BIZARRE. SEDUCTIVE. An ungodly dreamscape frozen in time—Death Hollow is at once grotesque and beautiful, foreboding and alluring, snaking its way through an ever-darkening abyss. Its massive domes are reminiscent of Yosemite, reflecting light and color in a peculiar way that suggests illumination from within. The gaping crevice tunnels its way through gleaming white sandstone, bound for the Escalante, the Colorado, eventually the Sea of Cortez.

In the desert, the story is always the same: water—finding its way, penetrating its path of least resistance through sand and stone, to the ocean at last.

Nature's paradox: the thing that shapes the desert is what it lacks the most.

I've walked miles to get here, over slickrock passes and scarped ravines, eventually descending a precipitous path along a 600-foot cliff. The crude trail was created over a hundred years ago, for horses. Horses? Riding a horse *here* seems implausible, yet somehow they managed a way down this primitive route—from Boulder, Utah, down into the murky depths of Death Hollow, then back up the bleached sandstone to Escalante—the only link connecting Boulder to the outside world. *The Mail Route,* as they called it, back before the assembly of roads.

Boulder must have been some isolated town. An old telephone line, a single strand of rusty wire, is still anchored to weathered pines, in some places lying on the ground, yet still somehow intact. A message from the not so distant past, of a simpler time, when adventure was a way of life.

The job description of *mail carrier* has certainly changed since 1909. Back then there were many such jobs, jobs that *required* adventure. Instead of traffic jams, these people navigated rugged landscapes, unpredictable weather, and the general uncertainty of the wild. We've civilized ourselves quite well, removing ourselves almost entirely from the natural landscape, all for the modern comforts of civilization. It's no wonder we're so restless.

These wild places were a part of us for generations. They're in our blood.

Just being outside changes everything. Cooking, cleaning, gathering water, setting up and breaking down camp—these activities are not just means to an end, but part of the overall experience. I'm peacefully unhurried. There is no urgency, no race against the clock, so I relax into *doing* as the experience itself. No more *preparing* for the moment. Everything is the moment.

I try this at home but fail. There's always somewhere I'm trying to be, running toward a future that never comes. Because I'm too busy preparing, racing toward peace and contentment. Now, peace and contentment consume every waking moment.

Ominous clouds. Whipping wind. Feelings of radical inclusion, grand indifference. Everything is starkly equal. I could fall from a cliff or be struck by lightning and nothing would change. No ambulances, no sirens, no helicopters. No onlookers, no traffic jams. No story on the evening news. Just the whipping wind. These fallen strands of wire. These ominous clouds.

Grand indifference. I find peace in that. Put in my proper place. No religion, no philosophy, just plain, simple, hard fact. Unobscured reality. A refreshing escape from the everyday illusion of our modern world.

The cold truth is—we don't matter. No more than a bug, a rock, or a tree matters. In this vast inclusiveness, we are all equal parts. And this is entirely the point, to be part of the shebang. Not to live separate closed-off lives, or to live the longest, or acquire the most, or domesticate the Earth, but to be part of the whole experience. To suggest otherwise is simple delusion.

Wilderness is not some vacation, some fairyland, some place of refuge from the real world. Wilderness *is* the real world. Earth in its natural state—before we got our filthy hands on it.

In wilderness, we are immersed in truth. It becomes abundantly clear that our pain derives from our false sense of separation. Here, that separation is utterly and completely gone—gone like a bad dream. We're returned to our natural order and place in the world. No better, no worse, but equal to everything else.

With this grand indifference comes radical inclusion and I feel only love—for the plants and flowers, chipmunks and hummingbirds, snakes and scorpions, seeps and springs, the passing clouds and the rays of sunlight—my kin. Like a long lost brother, I'm welcomed home.

To feel this in our civilized world is nearly impossible. Our feelings of separateness are so prevalent that they're contagious. Even if we practice yoga, or meditate, or pray—feeling one with the infinite universe for a few blissful uninterrupted moments—our feelings of separateness creep right back in through the back door. In a world where everyone feels separate, it's simply too much to overcome. But here I'm surrounded by trees, and they are enlightened! And the rocks—enlightened! Among them, my state of disconnect is the exception, and I'm attuned to broader perspective. Welcomed to a new world.

In attempting to connect us all through electronics, we have succeeded in universal disconnect. The constant alerts that beg every last drop of attention rob us from any connection we had in the first place. We are constantly being whisked away. The moment has been lost. We are all trying to find it. Searching for the only thing we know is truly real.

Now I find myself driving ten hours to Escalante, hiking ten miles into a remote canyon, so that I might finally grasp some reality. This, of course, is insane. But the journey proves worthwhile each time, because *here* lies reality in all its glory! Free from the constant buzz of civilization, I can finally feel my place in the world. And there is nothing really spiritual about it at all. Just plain simple honest truth.

What we need is a revolution. A paradigm shift. A breakaway from technology and a re-connection with the natural world. For when we disconnect we reconnect— with the truth of who we are.

Nature will welcome us back, as she always does with open arms. We are part of her as she is of us. Her love is so deep that it overflows our hearts, spreading out into the rest of the world. But don't take my word for it—I'm just a student. Go see for yourself. Leave your electronics at home, hike down into a remote canyon and sit, listen, wait. You may not feel anything at first, but just keep sitting. Listening. Waiting. Eventually, after a few hours perhaps, a few days, a few weeks, you may start to feel something.

Shhh...
Listen...
It's in the rocks. The trees. The wind.

Don't make sense of it. Don't try to put it into words. Just listen. Truth is silly, wise, profound. Nature speaks a simple language that gets right to the point. Listen not with your ears, but with your heart. Feel the love grow, then reciprocate. When you reciprocate the love grows stronger, overflowing with truth. Just keep sitting. Listening. Waiting. Soon, all feelings of separateness will dissolve, as you reconnect with the world you were born into. The one deep inside you know is real.

CHAPTER TWO

Dirty Devil Wilderness, Utah

A DUST DEVIL FOLLOWS ME, ablaze with evening light, as I drive down a sandy road just south of Hanksville. I ramble ten miles through sagebrush, the land looking like Kansas—flat as a pancake. A road to nowhere.

I keep driving, one hand on the wheel, the other trying to manage the exploding beer I've regrettably opened. The sun sets through storm clouds to the west but a few rays manage to peek through, casting an orange glow on the dust, the sagebrush, my foaming beer.

The road turns to deep sand and my truck begins to float, no longer banging and knocking all around, but surfing quietly now, like we're hovering three feet above the desert floor. I continue on like this for miles, beach cruising without the sea, until I notice the ground ahead dropping off into oblivion. Land's end. I hit the brakes and pause at the edge of a cliff. The dust cloud rushes forward, engulfs, dissipates—leaving me sitting at the edge of an abyss. After the miles of rolling sagebrush, I feel like I'm staring at the Grand Canyon: buttes upon buttes, layers under layers, canyons within canyons. I can barely make out the gleam of the Dirty Devil River over a thousand feet below. Water—good sign.

Oddly enough there are people: half a dozen Sprinter vans line the cliff's edge. A camera crew are filming two naked women poised on the canyon rim. They've timed this perfectly, not just for my unplanned arrival, but to catch the last rays of sunlight illuminating the women's bare, sun-kissed skin. The girls pay me no mind, neither do their photographers snapping away frantically with their Nikons, racing to capture the last of the fading light. The women must be freezing, their supple skin powdered in the fine crystals of blowing sand—but they don't show it. The images will be stunning, I'm sure.

I drive on, not wishing to interrupt the set. A little further down the road, still on the edge of the canyon but out of sight of the crew, I pull off onto a slab of sandstone to make camp.

Fetching leftovers from the cooler—pulled pork and mashed potatoes—I reheat last night's dinner on my tiny backpacking stove. Then crack another beer and eat heartily. This will be my last meal for five days.

In the morning I load my pack with everything but food: camping gear, rope, miscellaneous books, journal, pen—plus coffee and tea—*I'm fasting... not psychotic.* The trip will be a test, an experiment on my own body, to see how it can survive without food—as per original design—for times when supplies were scarce. Before grocery stores, refrigerators, restaurants.

I wish to empty myself of all distractions. The mood swings, cravings, and hunger pangs—I expect them, welcome them even. If I'm hungry, let me be hungry. Just let me be awake.

Well, lofty ambitions.

I may just go hungry. Grumbling stomach, lightheadedness, nausea, shaking, general unpleasantness. But I welcome those feelings too. If I wanted a vacation in the traditional sense, I would have gone to the beach. But driving out into the middle of the desert, all alone, to starve myself for five days—isn't it a bit much?

"It isn't logical. It's pathological," said Ed Abbey.

So why do it? What on earth am I asking of this life? Why not stay in the city where things are easy? Food, shelter, and basic necessities fulfilled for a fraction of my earnings. The rest spent on frivolous things—like books, for example.

We Americans are a spoiled breed, complaining about money yet rarely—if ever—going without food or shelter. I want to know how I function when the next meal is uncertain. We were designed to survive without super-markets, minimarts, fast-food chains. Does having our basic necessities constantly fulfilled make us happy? What do you do when every last desire is satisfied, every dream fulfilled?

Ask Robin Williams, Kate Spade, Anthony Bourdain...

With a light pack I stroll over open rock, leaving the upper world for the shadows below. I walk slowly, hunt-ing for routes. I drop a ledge, then another, lowering my pack each time with the rope. I'm losing elevation quickly, but the river still looks like a shoestring. My route takes me out onto a narrow ledge, about two feet wide—not much room for error—with a hundred foot cliff dropping to one side. Who made these routes? Who was the first? The earliest were likely animals, sniffing their way toward water. The faint footpaths of coyote, bobcat, deer, mountain lion. Navigation by smell must have been the way—trial and error, one dead end after another—until a path was revealed.

The route deteriorates. I find myself navigating more like an animal. Surveying for clues, hidden passages to the next level. I wander into the shade of an alcove and find dripping water—no more than a leaky faucet; filling a bottle here could take hours, the spring above accessible for a bird, a lizard, something that can scale vertical walls, but not for a human. I continue on—toward the muddy river.

Clouds darken, turbulent skies threaten weather. This is not a good place for a storm—clinging to the edge of this cliff like a clawless cat. Thunder cracks, a few raindrops fall, then stillness. I leave the main route, inspecting a small side canyon for a place to wait out the weather. A little ways in I find a shallow pool and a sandstone bench. With the approaching storms, I hunker down for the night.

Eighteen hours without food. I drink heartily from the pool, then make tea. I'm hungry, naturally, but my spirits are high, my energy levels steady. I'd prepared for this, skipping breakfasts, going on long day hikes without food, getting my body used to running off stored fat. My experiment is nothing original, no new fad nor diet.

Humans have fasted since the beginning of time. Sometimes for spiritual reasons, mostly out of necessity. Our bodies were designed to function for very long periods without food. We could not have survived as a species otherwise. Through most of history we were nomads, hunting and gathering, enduring harsh winters, traveling for days and weeks at a time searching for our next meal. It's only recently we came to eat three meals a day, snacks in between.

Now we eat compulsively, without thought.

We think we have freedom, but are we truly free? How many of us can choose what we want to do tomorrow? Most of us are locked into our schedules, chained to our routines. Freedom has become a myth, a distant dream, some ideological notion we long for, yet rarely obtain. Working through our prime sitting at desks, staring at computer screens, wasting away our youth so that someday, if we work hard enough, if we save enough, if the stock market doesn't crash, we might retire on a beach, or a cabin by the lake, or for those with less demanding tastes, in our own homes. Then, in our golden years, we shall finally have the freedom to do as we please, write our own schedules, live by our own rules—if we live that long, which is not certain.

Can't I live while I'm young?

I want freedom now. Is that too much to ask? In my golden years, I might be perfectly content with a comfortable chair. Is that what we're working so hard to obtain? A comfortable chair?

Must we eternally dwell in fear of early death, while simultaneously fearing a life too long? We worry we will die early, missing out on all the things we long to do. Or that our money pile will run out, leaving us to starve elderly in the streets.

We've become paranoid, worrying about everything except for what's in front of us. Life happens now—it will never happen yesterday, and as we well know, tomorrow never comes. Until we realize this glaringly obvious fact, we'll continually be striving for something we can never have. Running in circles, chasing our own tails, working to make as much money as possible, so that *someday* we can finally be free.

Freedom is now. Once basic necessities are covered, it's time to go outside and play. Look to the chipmunks and squirrels, crows and ravens, dolphins and seals. Or simply watch your own pets. They will remind you that life is a celebration, meant to be *lived*.

Morning.

My route takes me down off a ledge and into a jumble of rocks, dropping me the final 700 feet to the river. When I approach, the water looks like chocolate milk. No depth perception whatsoever. I scramble down the riverbank and slide into the murk. Clinging to tamarisk, I go waist deep but cannot touch the bottom. Kicking my feet frantically, I pull myself back onto the shore. How to discern depth without peering beneath the surface? There has got to be another way. I stash my pack, strip out of my clothes—no point in soaking everything.

Back into the water.

I sink to my chest, pretty deep, but the current is gentle, and I'm able to wade/swim to the other side. Success! But—I need to retrieve my gear. If I'd thought to bring along a trash bag, I could have floated my pack across—*it's the little things...* Now I'll need to find a shallower crossing.

Back into the water.

This time I zigzag my way through. Bracing myself against the cold water, I struggle for traction on the invisible floor, feeling my way through slurping sand, hidden rocks, twisted branches, until I find a path only waist deep—much better. I return to shore, shoulder my pack, then cross the new route without soaking everything.

The price you pay for solitude...

Now to dry off, slip back into my clothes, find—

I freeze. Abruptly, almost shockingly, my canyon emerges like an apparition, the materialization of a dream. I'd been too preoccupied to notice. Now my objective lies directly before me, a golden cathedral bathed in holy light.

What canyon? And why is *it* so special? Well, I suppose it's not special at all, at least in relative terms to any other. It has no popularity or fame, it won't make any top ten lists in *Backpacker* magazine—at least I hope not. Yet herein lies the allure—it's special only to me. The canyon *is* beautiful, yes, but no more than a thousand or so others. I chose it only because it looked lonely and obscure, difficult to reach. Something about the contour lines on the map—called to me.

Leaving the turbid river behind, I follow a broad tributary into deep sand, which quickly turns into rock. The walking is easy and soon water appears. The Dirty Devil was far too silty for consumption, so I'm eager to sample the cool clear liquid. I dip my bottle into the spring and bring it to my lips—salty—I spit it out and continue on. I hadn't expected this, but figure the water must get better upstream. At the next pool I stop for another sample— salty still—but less than the first. I continue several more miles, stopping periodically for samples until the water tastes clean and pure, then I fill up.

The stream is intermittent, flowing into deep pools, then drying up completely. Cottonwoods appear.

Then reeds. Blooming cactus flowers. A small tributary canyon joins from the west and I stop to navigate.

Alcatraz—depicts the map.

Sounds intriguing enough. I ditch my pack and stroll up Alcatraz. More cottonwoods, giant boulders with deep pockets of cold water. Lizards, frogs, tadpoles. Strange water bugs dart from my approach, dragonflies buzz here and there. The place is teeming with life. Beach vacations can be nice, but my paradise lies here in these lonely canyons. Delicate as a flower. Sweet as a lovely girl.

Afternoon.
Hungry. *Try to observe with curiosity.* Still hungry. I make tea. Shit—is the tea making me hungry? Dark and ominous clouds looming in the east. Sunlight creeping from behind the veil, kissing me with a breath of warmth. *Try to ignore this terrible hunger.*

Things will get better.
Must get better.

Desperation. Panic. Why am I doing this? Energy levels are high but desperation prevails. My tongue is the main problem—it's dry as cardboard. The more I drink the drier it gets. Plus I have this headache. I have clarity but the hunger will not pass. I drink more water, filling my stomach to capacity—still feel empty.

I. Am. Hungry.

Darkness.

Strange sensations throughout the night. Confusion. Low energy. Still in withdrawal from my sugar addiction, I suppose. I crawl out to face my demons. I've de-stressed all areas of my life. The noise, the lights, the concrete, the constant buzz of electronics, even the food—I've eliminated them all—now I don't know what I'm supposed to do. No clarity, no awareness, just an overall felling of irritation.

My first fasting trip was 25 years ago. Three days with just a bag of nuts. We were in the Chihuahuan Desert, on the border of Mexico, for an outdoor-leadership course. The nuts were there for reassurance; I would not be eating them. The solo was a requirement, one that I dreaded, fearing loneliness, boredom, *hunger*. I didn't understand the point of sitting alone, doing nothing—for three days! Why were they punishing us? This was supposed to be a *leadership* course, not solitary confinement.

Turns out, I actually *needed* solitude to peer beneath the surface. Certainly I experienced all the feelings I feared, but was somehow able to move through them. Rather than avoiding loneliness, avoiding boredom, avoiding hunger, I surrendered and became one with these sensations. I literally *was* hunger. And in that surrender I found freedom. I was liberated! And in control of my life for the very first time. When running from my demons was no longer an option, I faced them—and found only love.

Then the Earth spoke to me
Of magic and abundance.

Nights were exotic and full of mystery. Sunsets became dazzling and intense. I thought of my wife, Valerie, the two of us dancing both wildly and romantically in the sand, the sun setting down over the mountains. We made love like animals, under a billion stars, away from all the needless troubles and worries of the world. I realized that nothing else matters—all we need is love. And wilderness.

Morning.

I start coffee and stare up into the infinite sky—bright, blue, dazzling. I live my life high. Stimulated by sugar, food, caffeine, alcohol, serotonin, adrenaline. This extreme sobriety is jarring, and I can't seem to remedy the dry tongue. What's with the dry tongue? Why has it shriveled into a dead cactus?

Why am I forever infatuated with going deeper—constantly peeling back the linoleum, clawing through surface, trying to find some semblance of deeper meaning? Something to penetrate the illusion of our regimented world. Hunting for scraps of truth, morsels of magic, traces of wisdom, anything to prove we mustn't work so hard—just to be *okay*.

Where is the connection? Where's the joy? Is suffering all there is? I don't know that I can withstand another day of this. I want to explore but cannot seem to pull myself together. What is it that I must face?

Wind. Clouds. Dust and sand blowing all around. Must I die to be reborn? This is no longer hunger, it's something else. Uneasiness. A smile turned upside down.

Be patient, trust the process. Humans have fasted for millennia. I'm not alone.

Mother Nature, *show me the way...*

Evening.

Numbness. Powerlessness. My brain is weak, my heartbeat slow. Here I am in this beautiful canyon and I'm mildly bored. No connection at all. Sparks of emotion. Loneliness. Sadness. On the edge of crying but don't know why. Perhaps this is my metaphorical death. No future, no past, no joy. Just a rather sullen now.

The world stirs—traffic jams, accidents, murder, rape—but the desert sits, oblivious to the craziness. A cricket chirps, a bat flutters, and the sky grows silent with stars. A lone aspen sings her lonely song, inaudible to the rest of the world. Humans may have taken over the Earth, but these pockets, these sanctuaries, *remain*.

Starlit walls frame galaxies. Strange flashes in the heavens. Real or imagined? I'm not sure. Something is shifting—transitioning—from numbness to wonder. This fortress of magic is too lovely to be real. I must be awakening from some hazy dream. Reality is reclaiming its brilliance and truth, embracing me with love and light.

Eyes wide open.
The emerging clarity of a hunter.
Three days without food
And my heart is finally opening.

Listening deeply to the night, I almost forget to breathe. The desert sounds are so rich that every last drop of attention is required. To listen this intently is to be fully aware, each sound not just heard but grasped, understood, acknowledged. Between the sounds exists an ocean of silence, vast and infinite, as large as life itself. All-encompassing awareness, the essence of life—God.

The moon rises, casting silver patterns and shapes on the walls, gracing the canyon with whimsical light. The rocks scream their perpetual cry, resonating deeply inside my bones...

Stop! they proclaim. *What are you doing? What is your species trying to achieve? You have it all. You've made your lives comfortable, now go outside and play! There are sparkling mountains, dripping springs, twisting canyons. And they are all here for you!*

Morning.

Crystalline eyesight, explosive awareness, my mind as pure as a child at recess. Under the influence of none other than myself, the desert permeates me deeply, seeping into my pores, percolating through my veins, filling me with love, abundance, and gratitude for the boundless beauty of Earth.

I am here,
Not merely to survive,
But to live.

My lavish existence hits me like a freightliner. Three days? The longest I've ever gone without food? Laughable! How our first world problems pale in comparison to ever going hungry! A luxury most of us are born into without question. For most Americans, starvation has become a thing of the past. How often do we even consider our own abundance? Our meager troubles seem so trivial, so paltry. Yet it's comforting to know that the body will run on empty if it must—if our privileged existence should happen to change.

Strolling up the canyon, weather changes constantly, hot one moment, cold the next. Soon I enter a petrified forest with chunks of fossilized trees scattered about the desert floor—life immortalized in stone. For a moment I blend into my surroundings and forget myself completely. Craning my neck, I spy towering rock walls above, some corrugated, some smooth, others looking like Swiss cheese. The pools get deeper as I ascend, shaded by giant boulders and splintered logs, creating microclimates that never see the sun. When I look down into these pools

I find strange, ancient-looking crustaceans roaming about. In a rock wall sits a black cave—dark, haunting.

I lie down and stare up into morphing clouds, violent with chaotic brilliance. A lizard joins me and we sit together for a long while. There are insects all around but this is not meal time. She appears calm and peaceful. In a world where life eats life to survive, there must be an underlying peace. We are all going to die—enjoy it while it lasts. I admire the lizard's simplicity. No applying for jobs, saving for the future, putting kids through school. She sees a fly and eats it, then resumes her long day of lounging. The idle life of animals.

Our reality is different. You and I will likely never have to worry about finding food. Probably not shelter either. So we might have to declare bankruptcy, foreclose on our homes. Truth is, most of us can't afford where we live anyway. But really, what do we need? A place to sleep, cook food, and put our legs up at the end of the day? We make our lives so complex, so difficult to sustain, so damn expensive.

There is life outside the regiment. People are living it now, residing in tiny homes, or with no address at all, traveling on a shoestring. We are simply animals with large brains—we think too much, work too hard. With two legs we were born to roam and experience beauty, not sit behind desks and computer screens. We've done a great job creating our modern world. When is enough, enough? When can we celebrate our accomplishments?

It's time to take ourselves less seriously. Step outside the regiment and ask ourselves: What would be fun? We've created this marvelous society, when can we start living?

Morning.

I wake to a full moon with just a hint of dawn. I climb out from my slumber to witness the event. It seems the birds have the same idea, singing together in grand sonata, their tiny voices filling the canyons with song. Would the sun ever rise without birdsong? The sun obeys, playing her part, crawling slowly across the land until I'm bathed with light.

When the show is over the birds stop singing. Their job is done, the morning ritual over, the symphony ended. Do birds cause the sun to rise, or does the sun cause the birds to sing? Or is this just the big happening, everything linked together? One big organism?

Everything is as it is—without one we cannot have the other. So is the symphony of life. We are the eyes of the world, playing our own parts from our unique perspectives. How lucky we are to be part of the show.

It is our duty to live exciting lives, so that we might share our experiences with others, and inspire them to do the same. Is there any other logical explanation for our existence? Why on earth do we have such large brains?

To worry? To stress? To suffer? Or to play in ways creation never deemed possible? We can surf, ski, sail, sky dive, even scale vertical walls. We can cook incredible food laced with flavors beyond nature's wildest imaginations. We can make art, write books, create poetry, and express our unique perspectives of the world. We are evolving—from survivors to visionaries—so the world can express itself in ways like never before.

If we work ourselves to death—damming every river, paving every landscape, fencing every piece of land—where will future generations play? When we no longer serve a purpose, no longer appreciate natural beauty, and become nothing more than a parasite—the Earth will purify herself, as she's done so many times before.

When we eat ourselves to obesity, resorting only to our electronic devices for entertainment, gorging on images of death and violence while simultaneously pretending to shun both. When we become sloths, existing only to multiply, dominating every species, claiming every piece of God's green earth as *Private Property*. When we become a disease—we will be eradicated. Exterminated. Like a termite infestation. And the Earth shall go on without us, just as before, until a new species comes along. So the cycle continues.

I don't believe it's too late for the human race. We still have a chance. It only takes a shift. We are born knowing everything we need to know.

EAT
SLEEP
PLAY
LOVE

That's the formula. The rest of nature knows it well. And when animals grow old, they go off into the woods to die—and this is not a problem. Why must we desire to live as long as possible? Why not live until life is no longer fun—then move on, leaving room for new birth, so that they too might enjoy Earth's amazing wonders, as have we? Death is natural, just like birth, and there is nothing *wrong* with it. It's living for the sake of living that causes pain. When we learn to celebrate life and move on, leaving the Earth just as we found it—others may do the same.

CHAPTER THREE

Organ Pipe Wilderness, Arizona

A N AIR FORCE JET SCREAMS across the sky, tearing at the silence, followed by another. Then another. In a few seconds the mechanical birds are gone. Desert stillness returns, but strange feelings remain. There is something very real happening here. Have I stumbled into a sanctuary or a war zone?

This is border country. In extreme southern Arizona, the Organ Pipe Cactus National Monument lies just a few miles north of the Mexican state of Sonora. Along the trail-less route I find discarded bottles, empty bean cans, and water caches: gallon-sized jugs arranged in a circle with childlike drawings on the sides. Rainbows, crosses, a yellow sun rising over a saguaro-studded valley.

I come across an old well—dry, creaking. There are old cabins, some still intact with rusty sinks, broken tiles, ripped linoleum. The structures date back to the 1930s, when mining and cattle ranching were prevalent. But this human highway has been used for millennia, as evidenced by broken pottery, rock art, seashells scattered about the desert floor. Ancient footpaths of hunters and gatherers are still used today for illegal immigration. The human race never stops moving.

We are all just passing through,
Struggling to live, destined to die.

I think I've stumbled onto a main artery. They come up through the valleys, where the creosote grows thick—risking their lives while I walk freely. My heart grows heavy, sinks into my stomach. A complex question: why should I walk freely while others do not? My privilege was inherited, long before I was even conceived, when my parents were born—this side of the line. I'm grateful to be an American, but borders make me uneasy. Chained to our pasts, haunted by things we cannot change—the race of our ancestors, the country of our birth, the genetics of our parents—we're forced to play the cards we are dealt, carrying these heavy loads on our backs for the rest of

ORGAN PIPE WILDERNESS, ARIZONA | 43

our lives. Only the animals run free—unhindered by borders, fences, walls, property lines—imaginary dividers that have no meaning, history that contains no relevance. I continue on, descending a rocky ravine down into a wash, then up the crumbling bank to the other side. The Bates Mountains loom ahead, their ghostly shadows creeping slowly across the land. We needn't seek the present moment in a place like this. We're forced into it. Instincts require us to be alert, aware of our surroundings. This is not a stroll through a city park. I feel the need to be cautious. But is this all in my head? Immigration has been happening for generations. These desert travelers want nothing to do with me, simply wishing to get back to their families safely. "Just put yourself in their shoes," I remind myself.

We fear what we do not understand.

My mind drifts back to the water cache. Colorful rainbows, happy sunshines, little red hearts. But these travelers are real. At any moment we may cross paths. What will I do? What will I say? Will they ask for food and water? I have little to offer. My head stirs, spins out, collapses back in on itself, spiraling until there is nothing left.

We drift apart.
My mind and me.
One watching the other.

Who is this maddening, over-analyzing entity inside my head? Surely we cannot be related. But this disconnect is exactly what I needed. When we stop taking our thoughts so seriously, they lose their power, trailing off into some kind of distant background noise. Now there's nothing left but my footsteps, my steady beating heart. Nature passes no judgment.

We are all just passing through,
Struggling to live, destined to die.

CHAPTER FOUR

Glen Canyon, Utah

WATER DROPLETS DANCE around in a frenzy, appearing like snowflakes in the wind. With no rain in the forecast I continue on, through the mist, deeper into the narrows.

A rusty culvert marked an unlikely place to begin a journey, but first impressions can be deceiving. The drainage was just a portal—an obscure entrance to another world. For a mile I follow the crumbling ravine until it gives way to sinuous stone, dropping me into the bowels of the earth.

Deep below the surface, with just a sliver of blue overhead, I contort my body through spiraling tunnels and earthen cavities—down, down, down—until reaching a dryfall. A thirty-foot plunge. Dead end.

Without ropes, I'll need to go around. There are no straight lines in nature. Our survival depends on our willingness to adapt. So retracing my footsteps, I travel back up through the narrows, seeking another way. In a few hundred yards a terraced side canyon suggests a route. I take it—following crude footholds chiseled into the rock, up to the canyon rim, before sliding down a sandstone ramp, back to the underworld. Swallowed again by the chasm.

The dead end was just a detour, a signpost. Life is full of them; they guide us along, keep us on the right path.

After miles of parched sand, a spring appears, percolating straight up out of the ground. I'm mystified by its abrupt appearance, grateful for its arrival. Reliable drinking water changes everything, bringing much peace to the desert wanderer. I follow the spring as it gathers into a creek, leading me to a forest of cottonwoods—black trunks with neon leaves, glowing as sunlight slices its way through thermal cracks in the sandstone walls. The canyon makes wide meanders, creating rock houses, amphitheaters, domes.

Wading through ankle deep water, I navigate a subterranean corridor of warped rock and hanging gardens. The water deepens, covering my knees. Beaver dams appear, splintered trees gnawed at both ends.

Prints are everywhere, but as usual, the beavers fail to appear, hiding out in their solitary chambers.

The floor shifts—sand to gravel, gravel to stone—the water cutting channels and grooves in the rock, forming natural waterslides flowing into tubs swirling like Jacuzzis. The deeper I go, the colder it gets. In this chamber without sunlight, my T-shirt and shorts are not enough, but I continue on, the narrowing slot far too enchanting to halt further exploration.

I go until I'm freezing, no longer able to feel my toes, and reluctantly turn back—reminded that as much as we feel in control, Mother Nature has the upper hand. She, like always, shall determine our fate.

Morning.

Blue skies, then clouds, then rain. I prepare coffee, pouring water into a cookpot I've owned for twenty years. *Twenty years*—half a lifetime. It hardly seems fathomable. To justify the timespan I must stop, reflect—*boot up the old computer*—rekindling memories, stories, events. When the thinking stops the slideshow fades, past dissolves into present. Twenty years ago... Now.

Perhaps this is what makes us unique—our stories. Nature knows no history books, no photo albums, no sentimental cookpots. Everything is perpetually new.

The sun rises, the sun sets. Seasons come and go. Everything lives and dies without a story. Until someone comes along to write it down.

CHAPTER FIVE

Welcome to the Wilderness!

"**W**ELCOME TO THE WILDERNESS!" shouts a young couple from across the rapids. The last time I crossed Sycamore Creek it was bone dry—that was in the fall. Now being spring, it's blossomed into a raging river. I holler back, returning the welcome.

The crossing looks intimidating: whitewater swells and crashes over sharp boulders and rocks. But the couple cheers us across as we step out into the current, offering Valerie and me a hand here and there, until we make it safely through. On the opposite shore, the four of us sit on warm rocks and eat lunch, discussing plans, reveling in our good fortune. The couple is doing a long ambitious

circumnavigation of the area. We are just kind of mucking about—backpacking into the heart of the wilderness, setting up a base camp, and exploring from there.
Lollygagging by the shore, we finish lunch, then part
ways. "Happy wandering!" we holler through the pines
as we begin our ascent into the cliffs. "Adios, amigos!"
echoes back at us from below, drowned out by the roar
of rapids, the rustle of branches, the rattle of pinecones.

I follow Valerie into the trees as we skirt Sycamore
Creek for about a mile before climbing high into the bluffs,
leaving the creek inaccessible far below. The place looks
like Sedona, but without the pink jeeps and helicopters.
The canyon is wide, several miles across in areas, with
forests of sycamore trees that seem to glow from within,
haunting the desert with ghostly luminescence.

After a long day of hiking, we find a secluded camp in
the bluffs, far off-trail, and far from water. After pitching
camp, I hike back to a small pool I noted about a mile
back. Not much there—but I manage to extract enough
for the night.

In the morning we explore a narrow side canyon and find several large clear pools. Taking our
time to examine the many species of water bugs,
we spend most of the afternoon by water. Lazy day,
just as planned. Then, returning to camp with plentiful
water, we make dinner and sleep another night.

Welcome to the wilderness!

Recalling the words from the friendly couple back at the crossing, their sentiment echoes through my consciousness. Wilderness is indeed the destination, and there's nowhere we'd rather be. This gives us great comfort, being in the right place at the right time, an alignment of our world and the great universe. Our situation feels decadent—doing as we please, wandering at will, doing nothing as we see fit.

The foresight to preserve these wild places must be the most admirable endeavor civilized man has pulled off as of yet. Setting aside profit to preserve well-being? It seems so unlikely, yet here we are, reveling in the vastness of protected land, preserved for generations to come. A refuge from the chaos. A place to explore and feel our freedom. We mustn't take these wild places for granted—they may be the most valuable resources we have.

CHAPTER SIX

The North Cascades, Washington

OUR OLD TRUCK CREAKS and groans up the one-lane road, leaving German-themed Leavenworth, passing through old-growth firs, hemlocks, and cedars, toward the Little Wenatchee River. A station wagon approaches from the other direction and we pull over. The family stops, rolls down their window, informs us there's a bear up ahead—near the trailhead.

"Thanks for the heads-up," we say and continue on through the dark forest. When we pull into the trailhead we find no bear. Instead Valerie is greeted by a long, shiny black snake. She opens her door and it slithers away silently into the brush.

We fix lunch on the tailgate, organize a week of provisions, then head off into the deep north woods. The canopy is thick, damp, tangled. We slog up Cady Creek, bushwhacking through dense fern gardens, splashing through misty creeks. Mushrooms poke their heads up out of the mud, growing right in the middle of the trail. The foliage is so overgrown we cannot see our feet—the place looks like prime territory for *Ursus americanus*.

Now and then we utter a loud *whoop!* warning any beasts of our approach. It's not the black bear we're worried about, it's the infamous grizzly. We were warned by rangers about a small population living in the area.

The terrain gets steep, traction wanes on the slick mud and wet roots, but the constant buzz of flies and mosquitos keeps us moving. The ground slurps at our feet, tugging at our boots as springs percolate from the ground. Trees drip with dew, forcing us into rain gear to avoid getting soaked.

We plow on—enduring the mud, the flies, the mosquitos—because we know what lies ahead: the section of the Pacific Crest Trail that runs through the Henry M. Jackson and Glacier Peak Wilderness is legendary. It hugs the ridgeline of the Cascades for miles, traversing sprawling meadows and blue lakes, spruce forests with airy views, lofty peaks and rolling tundra. But we need to get there first. The only way to see it is to walk, as we are so well adapted to do, on our own two feet.

Anything you might see from a road is futile at best, like gazing through a restaurant window, hoping to taste the food.

Just before sunset, we reach the intersection of the Pacific Crest Trail. There we find a small flat meadow, the first decent place to camp. As luck would have it, water sources disappeared several miles back—no way were we going to camp in all the mud and flies and mosquitos down in the gorges. So leaving Valerie to arrange camp, I set off on a water hunt. Free at last from the weight of my pack, I bound through the woods like a rabbit, dashing off into the sunset. As I climb higher, the Cascade Mountains begin to come into view. A low glow radiates from the peaks, misty clouds settle into darkening valleys, and I slow my pace, creeping between roots, rocks, ravines. I carry a headlamp but leave it switched off, allowing my night vision to settle in naturally. I'll use the apparatus only if needed, for strange sounds in the brush.

I'm enjoying this immensely, hiking through the dark woods, out on the hunt. How far shall I go? Far as it takes. We must have water, and there was plenty in the gorges below. How far can it be? I cross a ravine, then another. Then another. For the love of God, there has got to be water. This is the Cascades! If I can't find it here, I've officially failed as an outdoorsman. I'll go until I find water and that is that.

Whistling through the dark, I announce my presence to any bears that might be frolicking up ahead. Then I climb another pass and find some snow fields glittering in the starlight. Bingo. I approach the drifts and find a small stream trickling out from beneath them, forming a tiny string of waterfalls gurgling down the side of the mountain. I thank Mother Nature for her bounty, fill my water bags, and scamper on back to camp.

When I arrive it's late and Valerie is already asleep in the tent. I gently rouse her, speaking softly of the water, the glittering snow, the mountains and starlight. Despite my exuberance she's reluctant, cozy in her bag, and doesn't want to get up. But once I have Thai curry sizzling on the stove, she's awake and alert. I hand her a steaming mug of tea and we huddle together, gazing at the stars, waiting for our meal to finish cooking. When dinner is ready, we enjoy our feast in absolute stillness, under a moonless sky and a thousand galaxies.

We sleep like stones late into the next morning, until awakened by footsteps. Thru-hikers on the Pacific Crest Trail are on the move, headed south, bound for Oregon, California, Mexico. We kiss and roll over—drift back to sleep.

After brunch, we hike on to Lake Sally Ann. There we meet a young girl who's been on the trail for four months. She talks about all the planning required for the long trek from Canada to Mexico: shipping boxes to resupply points, stopping in towns for a meal and a shower, tending to injuries along the way. I ask if she's seen any bears. Just one, she says—black bear, skittish and afraid. Attacks are rare. It's amazing really, that we fear these creatures at all. Here we are at the top of the food chain, successfully having killed off mastodons, saber-toothed tigers, marsupial lions, and now we are afraid of bears?

Newsflash: Bears are afraid of *us*.

The only thing humans have left to fear is other humans. Yet even that threat has diminished considerably. Despite what you may hear on the evening news, statistics show we are more susceptible to suicide than murder. Making our single biggest threat *ourselves*. A sobering thought.

Many would say that today, money is our biggest fear—or the lack thereof. The almighty dollar that we clench onto so tightly with both fists. Scraps of paper with no intrinsic value at all. Rational or not?

What would happen if you lost your money?

All your money?

There was a time in American history when losing your money meant you could literally die. Death by freezing or starvation was a real, actual threat. But today, very few Americans would actually starve or freeze to death if they lost their money. Even low paying jobs provide enough for basic necessities.

Note: cell phones, internet, Netflix, and cars are not basic necessities.

If you are injured and cannot work, we even have government programs that protect you from starving or going homeless. Our fear of losing money is only rational in the sense that our current standard of living may be affected, and even so, just temporarily. It's a well-known fact that many entrepreneurs go bankrupt several times over before finally making their fortune. After all, this is America. If starting a new business meant risking your life, and your family's life, no one would do it.

So if we needn't fear bears, or starvation, or murder, or loss of money, what's left?

Good question.

We exist at a time in history when living is easier than ever before. So go ahead, take risks, derail your routine, do something amazing. Our species has it made. We're no longer fighting off predators, battling other tribes, or freezing to death. What exactly are we doing working forty, sixty, eighty hours a week—just to make *a living*?

If there is anything to fear, it is time. Money can be replaced, time cannot. You can never get back lost time— time is *priceless*.

We leave the lake and are treated to meadow after meadow of pristine ridgeline walking. Views of velvety peaks extend in all directions. This is why we've come to the Cascades, to be delighted again and again by beauty beyond compare. To witness the finest scenery this planet has to offer, and to relish in the fact that day after day we will spend nothing for this amazement. It's astounding, all the little insignificant things that add up in the city, the money we throw away on this and that. In wilderness we don't spend a dime, and the longer we stay the more we save.

Five-star campsites abound. Grassy knolls with scattered trees and exploding views. We want to camp at every spot, but hike as far as we can before landing on one too irresistible to pass by. Perched on an island in the sky with

360-degree views of the mighty Cascades, we camp among trees covered in moss resembling wizards' beards. At once, Valerie and I lock eyes and name them the *Wizard Trees*. They look old and wise, comforting, watching over us, keeping us safe, providing some local company.

A fellow hiker passes through, heading off cross-country to climb a peak. We chat for a bit—he tells us he's out here for five days, sort of mucking about, exploring this and that, nothing particular in mind. We get along nicely, cut from the same cloth. His clothes are filthy, his beard ridiculous, yet his demeanor is relaxed and confident, unhurried. He knows the area well, eager to divulge his secrets before heading up to climb his peak.

The sun works its evening magic and the clouds join in, changing to cotton candy. The meadows follow suit, turning from green, to gold, to red velveteen. Then fading, fading, fading into darkness.

Morning.

Raindrops pattering the tent. Silent lightning. I climb out to get the fire going. The smoke is rich, enchanting. This is the kind of day that I'm grateful for no plans. It's the perfect day for lounging. If it storms we'll snuggle with the thunder. Or we'll piddle around the fire drinking tea, reading books.

The fire crackles, thunder booms, clouds darken. Occasional showers with slivers of light piercing through, drenching random peaks in pools of diamond light. We watch by the warm glow of the fire until the matinee is over, and the purple curtain falls.

Not a dead tree nor wilting flower is to be found in the lush and vibrant Cascades. Everything is alive and exuberant. All but the highest peaks are luxuriously carpeted, glowing green in any kind of light. Delicate mists swirl and twirl, dancing in the light. A single bolt strikes close as silence dangles by a thread, the two of us hunched together, anticipating the crash. Life suspended in time.

If there were no mountains, where would we go to experience such magic? Would every last piece of land be civilized, colonized, industrialized, privatized? Would solitude, reprieve, and salvation be forever lost? There are times when we *must* get away—that's why I'm so grateful for the mountains. Places of sanctuary. Where we will not be judged, criticized, or expected to live any certain way. Where we can simply be—who we are.

The breeze caresses our faces with the touch of silk. Rays of light squeeze between the clouds, illuminating the pale faces of the Wizard Trees. They look like old versions of ourselves—that's when we've truly arrived—when we see ourselves in others, accept our impermanence, dissolve into oneness, succumb to mortality. We are born to live in ecstasy, vibrating with the rest of nature. But removed as we are, we rarely experience this pure and blissful state of organic expression.

Mother Nature is pleading for us to get outside, back where we belong, before it's too late. Before we tame, conquer, and destroy the very beauty that is our birthright. We are meant to live in the Garden of Eden—all else is secondary, details, fluff.

Fluff. We love fluff. Fluff is great and fine and wonderful—if treated as such. So long as we remember the truth of our own identities, that first and foremost we are part of nature, connected to the mountains and deserts, rivers and streams, forests and plains, animals and plants— and to each other. Windows unto the world, essential parts of the whole, vital elements of consciousness.

You are here on Earth to fulfill a fundamental task: to be 100 percent uniquely you. No matter what you do with your life, your perspective matters. That's why you're here. Your perspective, for better or worse, is something we can all learn from. You make the world a better place, in ways you cannot even imagine.

How did we become so lucky to be a part of the cosmos? Frolicking the heavens, free to safely roam through beauty, magic, splendor!

The sky rumbles, the earth shakes, but still no rain. An owl hoots, a bird chirps, and razor-sharp nothingness in between. The raw piquancy of freedom lingers on our tongues; gratitude radiates from deep inside our bones.

We are free.

Freedom is not political, nor some religious belief or ideological concept. It's simply the privilege to walk, one foot in front of the other, in the direction of our choosing. Bound not by fences nor no-trespassing signs, only by our limits and desires. A freedom so pure you can taste it—existing outside our own self-imposed walls. It's out *there*, beyond the pavement, past the outskirts of town, toward that lovely brown sign that reads: Welcome to Your Public Lands.

When we no longer have a place to roam—to drink freely from our rivers and streams, and feast our eyes upon untrammeled beauty—freedom is lost, society doomed. When our natural landscapes disappear, suicide and depression will disease our youth and drug use will become the norm. Wilderness must be saved—our lives depend on it.

When we save wilderness,
We save ourselves.

Evening.

Fog rolls in, flooding the ridgeline with waves of mist dense as snow, blanketing the tundra, obscuring the landscape. We'd forgotten that blue skies are the exception this far north. This is the Pacific Northwest: the Cascades wouldn't be the Cascades without the fog. This is precisely why we travel: to be mystified by the glory of Mother Nature in ways like never before.

Enshrouded by mountains in the mist, the landscape disappears entirely as showers release from the sky, spraying our tent in sheets of tiny droplets as we dream away the afternoon. Rain invokes the deepest and wildest of dreams, as if being engulfed in total sound strips away the last fragments of consciousness, allowing us to drift effortlessly into the strange worlds of our imaginations. How curious that when we leave one reality, our minds quickly conjure up new ones. Constant entertainment is what our minds crave. Never a dull moment.

Morning.

The rain stops but the fog remains. Clouds rip past, coating our camp in fine mist. Occasionally the sky opens up—revealing freshly dusted peaks of gleaming snow—before filling back in again, isolating us to a floating isle in the clouds. With isolation comes invitation—we go inward. Vast landscapes overwhelm us with outward stimulation. Isolation takes on much different character, causing us to reflect deeply into our own souls, soaking up the serenity drifting in on the clouds.

The winds gust, blasting us with ferocious sound, then cease. A deer ambles up valley into our camp, pausing a few feet from the fire. We make no sound, neither does the deer, and the three of us hang in silence. When I reach for my tea he spooks, dashing off into the mist. This place belongs to the animals. Marmots are everywhere, reluctant to move if we approach. Owls hoot above our heads and the bears—which we've still not seen—stand their guard, snorting rather than running. They have the right. We've taken the rest, let them have theirs—what little remains.

A pillow of emptiness wraps, embraces, holds us warmly in its grip. Oh, to be free from the clutter of the mind! We relish in this bliss which is so rare, yet effortless up here in the clouds. I check my mind again, just to be sure, inspecting it from all angles. Nothing whatsoever—the cobwebs have been cleared. I fall into gratitude, for this experience, this life, this incarnation, this vantage from which only I can see.

How incredible that we get to see the world through our unique pair of eyes! Though now I realize, as the fog settles, that I am not only seeing through my own eyes, but through all the eyes of the world. The deer, the marmot, the bear, the shiny black snake—all windows into life through which we collectively look. How lovely to see through them all.

When the last drops of thought have fallen,
We are able to truly see
Through the eyes of the world.

We're all in this grand 'ole collective consciousness together. The sooner we understand, the sooner we will evolve.

In our cities of commerce and competition, the rat race pursuit of money and power seems to make sense. Up here it seems like insanity. Sit upon this hillside and you shall see that all is connected, intrinsic parts of the whole, organs of the same body. If the lungs were to fight with the liver, we'd call it disease, yet we compete with one another every day and think nothing of it.

We stay the entire day—drinking tea, contemplating existence, wasting time, going *nowhere*. When you're always busy going somewhere, nowhere seems a nice place to be.

Valerie is content reading, and I decide to go for a hike up Foam Creek. Once off the main trail, the wilderness immediately feels different. Because this faint path fizzles out in just a few miles, and doesn't connect or form any kind of loop, it is deserted. Wildlife seems to know this, flourishing in solitary abundance. Marmots run up ahead of me, poking their heads out from holes in the ground, whistling as I go by—jolly lads—swaggering around in their oversized coats, goofing off like schoolchildren. They appear curious, running and then hiding in the brush, popping up their heads, then running directly toward me for a better look, taunting me to engage in their silly game. They know us backpackers well, likely never having seen us run. Slowly we walk with our heavy loads, always on the move—even way up here—with our schedules, deadlines, ambitious goals, and restless pursuit of adventure. The most bang for the buck, in the least amount of time. The animals know very well that we are visitors just passing through.

I hike out to a rocky perch. Higher in elevation now, I can see above the clouds and the fog. Sunlight illuminates snowy peaks in the distance, the air is pleasantly cool, and layers of clouds roll beneath me like magic carpet. Immense calmness hovers in the air.

The hillside before me is covered in flowers. There's something about this filtered light that makes everything glow brighter than usual. I'm surrounded by a sensuous palette: red columbine, purple larkspur, tiny gardens barely noticeable until I really study them.

The ground is covered, not in grass but by tiny plants, glowing algae, and miniature forests of trees and bushes only millimeters in height. When I look closer, there are even smaller plants, astonishingly perfect in symmetry, with little flowers growing out of them.

If I had a microscope we could go even further, revealing cells and atoms, until we reach that all-consuming nothing that composes everything. That life stuff we are all made of.

There I find my truest self,
In all that nothingness.

What a great place to be. I know that when I die I will return to this place of nothingness. I'll lose this set of eyes but an infinite number will still remain. This is always the goal: to get down to nothing. Because in all this nothing lies the source of everything. And that dichotomy is extraordinarily exciting!

Want to know the meaning of life? Go watch kittens for about an hour, or puppies, or baby squirrels, or bear cubs, or small children. Of course they could never *tell* you the meaning of life. They can only show you—for the question would seem meaningless and irrelevant. "Who cares?" they would say. "Let's play!"

We are all born with playfulness—and play we will, until we're taught that life is serious. That there are very important things to be done, and that we must focus not on the present but on the future. "What do you want to do with your life?" we are asked. "No, not now," they insist, "in the future?" So begins the shift. Slowly we stop celebrating the glorious present and begin focusing on the future. And the *reason* for all of this? To be happy.

Not now, *silly*. In the future.

"Work hard now," they reason, "and you'll be happy later." Happiness is stolen from us, and placed in an imaginary future that we can never reach. We become lost in illusion, or rather disillusion: that happiness resides in the future. A practical joke we've played on ourselves.

But there is a way out. Come to the mountains. Come to the wilderness and the animals will remind you about the celebration of life. That once food and shelter are secured, celebration, beauty, and love are all we need. Love is everywhere, beaming from the trees, the sunlight, the clouds, the mist. We must only grab ahold of it and run wildly, out into the world with playful glee, celebrating the glory and splendor of life.

No guru. No method. No teacher. Just come to the mountains and the truth will find you. But if your mind is too busy you will never hear it. If you're always trying to get somewhere you will never get it. Because here and now is where it all lies.

On the fourth day, we leave the misty wonderland of the ridge and head back down into the flowers as more and more slivers of blue sky reveal themselves. Downward we go, traversing fifty-degree slopes draped in tapestries of purple and white. Down into the trees, through the old growth, across the gurgling streams, then up onto a bluff. Clouds have cleared, bluebird skies are back, and all day we hike, into the cool evening light. The sun sets and we settle down in a tranquil meadow. It's colder tonight and we are glad to be off the ridge, out of the wind. We spend another evening stargazing. The night is long and desolate.

Daybreak.

Skies are scoured clean and the sun shines with new warmth and brilliance! When we wake, our tent is drenched with dew, but the sun dries it within an hour.

We have only two days left, and as usual I can feel our trip winding down. So many dramatic scenes flash through my memory: wildflowers, wizards' beards, misty mountains, lofty ridges! But our trip is not over yet. Today we'll hike to Blue Lake, camp one last night on Cady Ridge, before making the long descent back to Little Wenatchee Creek. It's time to savor our final moments, enjoying every aspect of wilderness to the fullest.

Blue Lake.

This was supposed to be an easy hike, over to Blue Lake for a quick swim, then back to camp to relax away the remainder of the afternoon. Mother Nature had other plans. Climbing loose rock with little traction, we ascend a long exposed ridge, only to see Blue Lake looming far below a crumbling scree field. So it goes in the wilderness. We came to swim, so we push on—scrambling down the loose rock, toward the shimmering waters below.

The color of Blue Lake is stunning. There are many lakes with this common name—some blue, some not so blue. This one is blue as sapphire, fading into turquoise around the edges, with lush grass like a freshly manicured lawn. Five days without a shower and the scene looks delightful. The only thing better might be a taco stand and cold margaritas, but for now the lake will have to do.

The water is cold—crazy cold! But the day is warm, the skies clear—and we both take the plunge. Exhilarating, to say the least. A few seconds is all we can muster, and we finish bathing with washcloths on the sandy shore. It sure is nice to be clean.

After drying in the sun, we head down to a waterfall flowing from the lake and relax in the shade. The sounds of the cascades soothe us as we dine on mixed nuts and pepperoni. The food is divine, the spring water holy, our freshly cleansed bodies invigorated. *So it goes in the wilderness.* Nature intensifies the enjoyment of simple pleasures.

Engulfed in a field of Indian paintbrush, we relax into the indulgent feelings of gratitude. *Indulgent gratitude?* Sounds like an oxymoron, yet somehow, here, it seems possible. In town we must remind ourselves to be grateful, so we're not always craving the next thing. Here gratitude is the norm. We are simply grateful to be alive. The water has cleansed our minds, freeing us from desire. We are happy to be here, nothing else is required. Except perhaps those tacos...

But city life will come soon enough. Why tarnish the moment with our frivolous cravings? Buddhists say the end of suffering is the end of craving. How true that seems to be in wilderness. But you needn't become a monk to end craving, just come to the mountains and watch your desires drift away, like leaves on a fall day.

Last night on Cady Ridge.

We set up on Cady Ridge and stare out over the Cascades one final time. How we've gotten used to these five-star accommodations. We shall remember them fondly.

In the morning the mosquitos are thick and we pack up early. But what would have been a quick hike out is prolonged by the abundance of blueberry bushes along the trail. Picking the sweetest, plumpest of the lot, we stop around every corner, transforming our hike into a breakfast buffet.

With blue-stained fingers and lips, we travel once again through the old growth, through the mossy trees and ferns, across the Little Wenatchee River, and back out to the truck. No bears, no snakes, just some frosty beers waiting for us in the cooler. We crack a couple and toast to a glorious trip. It's barely noon, but when you're on mountain time...

CHAPTER SEVEN

Rainy Pass, Washington

SUNLIGHT SCATTERS through tall pines as we climb from Rainy Pass into the Okanogan-Wenatchee National Forest. Alongside warbling Porcupine Creek we scamper up the trail, eager to reach the magical world above the trees. When we reach the ridge we find a rocky ledge and set up camp. It's August, but it looks like winter as the sun sets behind distant snowy peaks. The highest mountains are enshrouded with cloud, but the sun still shines upon us, warming our bones as we settle in for the sunset, the blue moon, the jeweled night sky.

In the morning we do a little house cleaning: breathing with the wind, allowing the crisp mountain air to sweep any remaining dust from the far corners of our minds. This will make it easier to hear what the mountains have to say. If our minds are soiled with thought, we'll miss the message entirely. So we sit, breathe, cultivating awareness until we've had all the ecstasy we can take. Then we dash off into the woods.

We crest a pass and a new world unfolds. That's what's so enticing about passes; each reveals a previously hidden landscape. Entire mountain ranges come into view along this pathway in the sky. Above treeline the mountainsides steepen, plummeting a hundred feet only inches from where we walk. Not exactly for the faint of heart. We call this the no-fall-zone: you don't fall here—not an option. Along these steep sections we find it difficult to take in the views, so we must stop frequently and gaze up at the beauty that surrounds us.

Water emerges, tumbling down vertical ravines, then disappearing underground. These are the best drinking sources. Holding our water bottles directly under the faucet, we fill up with cool, sweet spring water, filtered by Mother Nature herself.

Good living: frolicking the frontiers of heaven, tasting the purest of waters, bathing in the holiest of light.

We pass another hiker and find him as enamored as we. "Can you believe this!?" he exclaims. "Ha!" Before we can respond he disappears around a corner like a phantom, along this earthen bridge in the sky.

Clouds drift in, draping entire peaks with shadow, then rippling through the trees with lacy patterns, texturing the landscape with depth.

We reach Methow Pass and abandon the trail, heading far into the meadows, and spend the night on a craggy ridge among dwarf pines and gardens of bitterroot, monkey flower, pussytoes. We make chili with spaghetti—Cincinnati style—then relax for the remainder of the afternoon.

At dusk, a small pygmy owl pays us a visit. Flying low he glides over our heads making no sound. Silent hunter of the night—the owl is a bird with the utmost style and grace. He stops several times at the treetops, silhouetted against the night sky, illuminated only by stars. He keeps us company for the rest of the evening, leaving us only when we fade into dreams.

We sleep until the wind shakes us from our slumber. I peek out and see winter clouds hovering over the highest peaks, settling down into the glaciers. We are cruising toward fall and I welcome it fondly. Goodbye mosquitos, hello golden days of autumn. Warm afternoons, frosty nights, the promise of fresh snow. It won't be long before we're floating on fluff, surfing the backcountry on skis, under sparkling skies with no crowds. The mountains will be cloaked in robes of diamonds, every valley waiting to be explored, every glade waiting to be carved. No trail, no problem. In winter, the entire mountain becomes our playground. But we mustn't get ahead of ourselves, snow will be here soon enough; for now I'll take this warm slice of granite, savoring the final days of autumn splendor.

We are products of our environment—our minds will latch onto anything. Exhausted by advertising, we are constantly persuaded to do this and desire that. No one is exempt and we are all to blame. I promote my books, your company promotes their services. We live in the highly sophisticated age of targeted advertising. And this is ll very well and fine and part of our culture. What's important is to recognize that our thoughts and cravings are not entirely our own. We are what surrounds us.

Change your surroundings,
Change your mind.

When returning from a wilderness trip, we see the world in a whole new light. A newfound sense of curiosity and humor evolves, because we realize our cravings are not who we are. Wilderness provides perspective, gives us a clean slate from which we may begin again—from the beginning.

The cycle repeats itself over and over. We remember who we are—we forget. It's easy to get lost in a sea of advertisements, telling us who we are and who we should be. What kind of house we *should* live in, what kind of car we *should* drive, what kind of furniture we *should* own, what kind of clothes we *should* wear, what kind of music we *should* listen to, what kind of food we *should* eat, so on and so forth.

It's not just peace of mind that wilderness offers, but freedom and independence. The opportunity to have thoughts that are entirely your own.

You mean, I shouldn't believe everything I think?

When we start to take our thoughts too seriously—this is when we lose grasp. We fall into disillusion, identifying ourselves with the complexities of the mind. The human brain was intended to be used as a tool, so that we could hunt, fish, gather nuts and berries, build shelters, fight off attackers—stay alive. But when there is no longer a need to hunt, or build our own homes, or fight, our minds begin to wander. *The tool has been left unattended.* Let it go too long and the brain becomes a monster—attaching itself to every whim, every desire, every problem, anything at all.

In wilderness we see the world as it truly is. Mountains, deserts, rolling plains, oceans with unfathomable depths, tropical islands and rainforests, animals, plants, and the Earth: a tiny speck of dust hurling through space, in a universe full of infinite galaxies. And all of this within an even larger void of all-consuming nothingness. This is reality. Not some idealistic fairytale version of the world, but the real actual truth. And it's spellbinding.

In wilderness, we see that our lives are utterly and completely meaningless. And in this we find meaning.

The lesson is always the same.

We are born, we have a life, we die. So is the circular nature of being. It happens over and over, and no one is exempt. Why not celebrate the inconceivable notion that we get to witness it all, through our own unique pair of eyes?

Our minds function differently in the wild, not because they are switched off, but rather they are switched on, finally put to intended use. Instead of wandering around aimlessly in mindless thought, our minds are highly alert, standing guard, charged and ready for any task. Solutions to problems come rapidly and without waver. The brain becomes a powerful tool, solving problems as they arise, then waiting silently—on-call—ready for the next task, as per original design.

The ability to think only when we wish has become a rare skill. When our minds are chronically clouded with meaningless worries and trivial concerns, they're per-petually exhausted. Then when a real problem arrives, we're overwhelmed with indecision. This leads to stress, procrastination, anxiety, and finally—if this sort of thing goes on too long—depression.

Watch a cat and you will see that she is highly alert. Her awareness not single-focused but extending out equally to all sides. Her hearing is keen, silently awaiting predator or prey—sitting, listening, waiting—ready to pounce, yet peaceful and tranquil at the same time. They've even learned to sleep in this state.

Our animal instincts are quite similar. They've not been lost but neglected, forgotten due to lack of use. Turn them back on and all cylinders fire up, racing back to life with the flick of a switch.

Sit in the forest long enough and you begin to see through animal eyes. As the fog of mindlessness starts to clear, thoughts flow away like water, cascading down the mountainsides into the valleys, seeping into the soil, deep into the core of the Earth to be purified, cleansed, reborn into the world. Beginning again as you did when you were a child, but with the knowledge and wisdom of age. Now you are free, ready for civilization.

Until *it* happens again.

We can only take so much civilization before it *gets* to us. Then it's time to get back to where it all begins.

Wash. Rinse. Repeat.

So is the cycle. Our civilized world is not reality, but a game we play. Existing so we can pack millions of us into a tiny area, complete with electricity and indoor plumbing, restaurants and beer gardens, movies and bookstores, cars, trucks, and busses, subways and airplanes. It exists for our amusement—and there is nothing *wrong* with it—so long as we realize that the real world is outside, with the rest of nature, and should be treated as such.

When we preserve wilderness we preserve what is real, natural, and essential to our health and well-being. Our very survival as a species depends on it. We cannot have society without wilderness any more than we can have flesh without bone. Without wilderness we create our own prison, boxing ourselves in from all sides.

Amusement parks are fun, so long as we may leave at closing time, lest we become locked inside, slaves to our own devices, trapped inside a video game of our own creation, with no possibility for escape. The game is fun, yes, but the fun quickly fades when we forget we are playing.

Morning.

Our view from camp overlooks the North Cascades: Black Peak, Boston Glacier, Inspiration Glacier, Forbidden Peak. Occasionally we lift our heads to view the sunrise over the mountains outside the tent door.

As usual, we're reluctant to leave, but the usual perks of the front country are creeping in: fish sandwiches, frosty beers, showers.

Our hike takes us back into deep forest and we soften our pace. We pass several small streams and waterfalls before rejoining Porcupine Creek, our final descent. In a couple of hours we are back to the car, washing up, cracking beers, packing away our gear, preparing for civilized life once again.

We stop for a swim in the Methow River, then hit the Old Schoolhouse Brewery for fish and chips on the patio.

After lunch we cruise the Methow Valley, stopping at local orchards for peaches, apples, tomatoes. We drive along the Okanogan River, through the quaint towns of Winthrop and Twisp, slowly melding back into the comforts and pleasantries of the front country—with newfound appreciation for it all.

CHAPTER EIGHT

Thank God for Public Land

OVER THE RIVER AND THROUGH THE WOODS, into the forest we go. Up the winding road, through the neighborhoods, past the outskirts, and final remnants of civilization: abandoned cars, boats, motorhomes, washing machines, refrigerators, piles of trash. And the usual foreboding signs: PRIVATE PROPERTY, NO TRESPASSING, KEEP OUT; BEWARE OF DOG, CAT, OWNER, GUN, EX-WIFE.

In another mile we pass the national forest boundary sign and immediately—like always—the rusty appliances, trash, and threatening signs vanish. Nothing but the whispering pines, the golden aspen leaves—swaying freely in the in the breeze.

Thank God for public land.

I let out the usual sigh. It's good to be back on free soil. The road becomes rough, steep, rutted—like all good roads—as we shift into low gear and take an unsigned spur on the right, then another, and yet another. Trees close in, brushing both sides of the truck like fingernails on a chalkboard. We squeeze through, stopping to remove larger branches from the road, then replacing them back behind us.

Leave No Trace—have no neighbors.

We climb higher, and higher still until the views open to a grassy meadow. We park amongst scattered pines, killing the engine, stepping out onto the soft dirt under the fat old sun. Then we lower the tailgate and crack a few beers. Taking Valerie's hand in mine, we watch the orange sunshine disappear over the North Cascades, the Pacific Crest Trail, the rolling hills of the Okanogan—everything dipped in golden evening light.

"You can't dream a place like this," I sigh.

"Just have to get lucky," Valerie says.

Ain't that the truth. Our national forests allow us to be explorers again, settlers of our own land, if just for the night.

Free land is what makes us free. A place to ramble, hunt, fish, or just camp on a grassy hill, drink a few beers, and fall asleep under the stars. Undecided, undefined, undisturbed. No fences, no signs, no fees, no reservations. No bullshit.

CHAPTER NINE

The Wallowas, Oregon

SLIPPING INTO DARKNESS, I pitch my tent under God's twinkling campfires ablaze in the heavens. The climb was worth it—life is always better above treeline. The Wallowas, meaning "land of winding water" to the native peoples of the Nez Percé, have been on my mind for as long as I can remember. In the northeast corner of Oregon, the mountain range is far from everything, with the exception of a quaint little town called Joseph. Situated on a mountain lake, Joseph has restaurants, breweries, hiking trails, and a rustic lodge by the shore. Valerie will be staying there, at the lodge, for a few days while I explore the wilderness. She needs a break and some creature comforts, I need to see the Eagle Cap Wilderness. She'll be happy, I'll be happy—so is the arrangement.

A couple must have the opportunity to miss each other—a vital element for a healthy marriage. Solos are good for the both of us, a ritual we perform at least a few times a year, just to keep the relationship pure.

There was a time when I *needed* solo trips—to preserve sanity—back when I worked a stressful job with long hours and too much time spent indoors. My life is much simpler now. Goodbye stuff—I don't need you anymore. I don't make much money these days, but I don't care. A carefree lifestyle takes some engineering, but I tell you it's possible.

Life is about moving toward where you want to go, and away from where you don't. I know that sounds overly simplistic but it's true. Years ago while on a solo trip in the Utah desert, I got really clear about what I wanted. On the back of an old business card I found in my pocket, I wrote:

1. *Explore wilderness.*
2. *Inspire others to protect it.*

I put the business card in my wallet and looked at it every day. From that day forward everything changed. I started basing all my decisions on what would move me toward where I wanted to go—the wilderness—and away from where I didn't—the office. I quickly realized that when you know what you want, the rest of life's needs get pretty simple. We need:

1. *Food to eat.*
2. *Water to drink.*
3. *A warm place to sleep.*

What a relief! You see, the problem with not knowing what you want is that you want everything. So we spend, spend, spend on every little thing we think will bring us happiness. Of course happiness never comes, because we never actually asked ourselves what we wanted in the first place. We're like ships sailing the open seas without a compass, changing course every time we think we see land.

Life is a harrowing adventure of ups and downs, twists and turns, intense joy and blood-curdling fear. The key is knowing how to steer the ship during the storms. If you don't know where you're headed, the storm may take you someplace you don't want to go. Storms can be opportunities, so long as you don't get stuck in the troughs. Troughs are necessary, but the crest will always come. That's when you need to be ready—or you'll miss your opportunity entirely. So is life—a wave that builds and crashes over and over again. The key is learning to surf. There's magic behind every swell, but if you're too oblivious to notice, you'll miss it every time.

Morning.

Life in the treetops. The Wallowas stretch out before me, silver in the morning light. Red columbine and pink tiger lilies dot the hillsides. Cool air, slight breeze, very few bugs.

I asked three backpackers at the trailhead yesterday how the bugs were. The first said *terrible*. The second said *not bad*. The third said *moderate*. I'd go with *moderate*, depending on choice of campsite. Camp by the lakes and you may get *terrible*. Camp in the breeze above the trees, and you'll get *not bad*. Life is subjective. We all have our perceptions. Many would call this entire outing *terrible*. Walking with a heavy pack, through mosquito-infested woods, for no reason? Nonsense. Why not enjoy a nice day at the spa, or a plush hotel with a view? Legitimate questions. But then I consider the cost of such excursions, requiring the working of longer hours, limiting the experience to maybe a weekend or just a few days. A hotel suite might be 500, 700, 900 square feet? My terrace above the trees is at least an acre, with unlimited room to roam on all sides, and unencumbered views all around. There is no nightly rate and I may stay as long as I wish, or change locations each night, my only limitations being my own stamina and desire.

Wilderness offers humans of all economic classes the opportunity for true adventure, transporting us to natural places of unimaginable beauty and splendor. Not to mention the spiritual benefits of such an outing: the sense of renewal and rebirth, the reminder of the very essence of our true nature. Not a vacation but a retreat, a ritual, an escape from the mundane—of everyday life.

Not that there is anything *wrong* with the plush resort or hotel spa, but how much sweeter are such luxuries after a few nights spent in the woods? How much more delicious the food tastes, the beer satisfies, the Jacuzzi relaxes.

The wilderness experience is a microcosm of life. There can be intense pleasure as well as intense discomfort. There are literal ups and downs, peaks and valleys, highs and lows. So is life. It's the ability to handle those peaks and valleys, and learn how to enjoy them for what they are, that is the lesson out here. We cannot have pleasure without pain; they are equal parts of the human experience. They give life context—could we ever know joy without anguish?

To avoid pain is to avoid life. Wilderness reminds us of these basic truths. You cannot step onto any one peak and stay there forever, nor would you want to. After a while you'd become bored. The only way to get to the next peak is back down into the valleys, the dark woods, the lonely forest—then it's another grueling climb back to the top.

Life is about change, not staying in one place all the time. Yet this is exactly what we tend to do. We find one level of happiness we are comfortable with and throw out the anchor, working our tails off to stay on that one peak, forgetting that we were born with two legs to roam, and the world is full of endless peaks!

It's no wonder we're so easily depressed. Our modern lifestyles go against every fiber of our beings. It's simply not possible to grab onto any one moment in time and stay there forever. Life moves. Time moves. If we fight it—we suffer.

Society clings onto a false sense of security. Life is insecure. Things change. Stuff happens. We can be laid off, lose our money, our houses, our cars, our possessions. So we work longer and longer hours, trying to hold onto some imaginary sense of security, knowing that in the end we are all going to die anyway. And no one, absolutely no one, can say when that is. Today? Tomorrow? Next week? Fifty years from now?

This is the joke—the big gag.

But if our fears are irrational, why do they consume so many? The answer is simple: we are products of our surroundings—if everyone feels a certain way, we do too.

Change your surroundings. Change your mind.

Go to the mountains and nature will remind you that society is not real but a game we forgot we were playing.

When we learn to enjoy the climb as much as standing on the peak, we are back into the flow. Life flows! When we surrender to the flow, every moment becomes more enjoyable. Things start to work out because we are no longer fighting our way upstream, but drifting with the current. Life becomes a joyful journey rather than a desperate search for more highs and less lows—which is like fighting life itself. When we surrender to the flow, we tune ourselves back in to nature.

But you know all of this. I know all of this. The problem is we forget. Over and over we forget. That's why wilderness is so important. We are students and Mother Nature is our teacher. We must never stop learning. Never stop attending the sermon. Forsake nature and you forsake yourself, renouncing your own mother, doomed to be eternally lost in the mindless pursuit of soulless desire—the great illusion of modern times.

My trail plummets a thousand feet, then another thousand. Rather than deep woods, I drop into an open basin as the Eagle River Valley explodes in living color, saturating my senses with wild, untamed beauty. Waterfalls erupt from ravines dressed in flowering bouquets of lupine, bellflower, larkspur. When I reach the bottom,

I know that I must regain all that I've lost, but this doesn't matter because the valley is massive, unveiling more earthen majesty as I descend the inner sanctum.

These are the Wallowas I've come to see! I'm reminded of the Uncompahgre, the Maroon Bells, the Wind Rivers. The country is rich and well-watered, with creeks flowing from every mountainside, and mesmerizing gardens ornamenting craggy granite walls.

I whistle with delight, gliding downhill, high on beauty, high on life. Alone in the mountains, yet surrounded by great company, so many friends I've come to know.

Many will never see such beauty—this breaks my heart, reminding me to always be appreciative for my health, my strong legs, and my short time on this Earth. With no one else around, I'm left alone to adore Mother Nature in her finest gowns, her most exquisite jewelry, entranced in a drunken state of rapture, mile after blissful mile.

The trail becomes overgrown as I'm engulfed in fields of lilies up to my shoulders. With no place to stop and rest on the marshy ground, I'm forced into constant movement. When I reach the foot of the valley, the trail switches abruptly back upwards toward the pass, reclaiming all the altitude I'd lost. My plan was to camp halfway up the pass, but the ground is far too steep so I keep climbing, ascending another thousand feet. Creeping up the mountain, my exhausted legs trudge along automatically—in the lowest possible gear—running on fumes. So is the program: one foot in front of the other. The wilderness does not care if we are tired. When there's nowhere to rest you keep moving, simple as that. One step at a time until you get there. Our bodies were specially designed for this—to run on automatic—walking for days, weeks, months if necessary, just as our ancestors did through all types of weather, stopping only when they found food, water, or a suitable place to stop for the night.

In another 500 feet my hopes rise. The ground starts to level out, there are flowing creeks and springs, and a steady breeze keeps the bugs away. The pass, now within striking distance, should be a fine place to spend the night. Towards the crest I find a granite terrace overlooking the wildflower valleys below. A large cirque sits behind, with three charming waterfalls adorning her vertiginous slopes. It sure is good to be home.

First things first—I go down to wash my filthy feet in the stream. Then I switch into camp clothes, set up the tent, and make hot tea. So is the ritual. As always, I want everything all at once, but I tackle my chores one at a time, carefully, systematically, allowing my body ample time to transition from work mode to rest. The many comforts of camp will be here soon enough.

Why am I so absent-minded at home? Fumbling around with chores, trying to make time go faster, rushing to get on to things I'd *rather* be doing. Here I'm relaxed and intentional, tackling even the most menial tasks with mindfulness and intent, savoring each movement, celebrating the complete event, not just certain elements. From cooking to cleaning to digging a hole for my morning shit, every moment is as rich and delightful as the next.

How I'd love to live like this all the time! But in the city I find it impossible, constantly being whisked away by desire and temptation, the next *better moment* just out of sight, lurking around the corner.

I'll be happy *when...*

Future moments keep presenting themselves and the present never comes—this is the problem. But here, I can't really get anywhere else. I can't go watch a movie, or drive to a restaurant, or buy something on the internet, so desire and temptation don't really exist. What I have is what I got.

If there is anything that causes suffering, it's our constant desire for something else. To feel different than we feel. To be somewhere other than where we are. We are constantly saying no to life, that it's not good enough, that we want something better.

Morning.

An early sunrise coaxes me from my steaming tent. I walk down to the water and allow the soothing stream to ease me into the day. A charming hummingbird inspects my red shirt, a steady breeze keeps the pesky vampires away, and another perfect morning ensues in the Wallowas.

Curious critters dash through the rocks. Pikas? Squirrels? They move so fast I cannot be sure. Heathery clouds airbrush the sky, veiling the sun, keeping the morning cool. I'm not ready for the heat of the day; better to savor these long mornings as much as possible. I could have woken earlier, but sleeping is yet another luxury, especially with the constant sound of water lulling me back to slumber, keeping me in that delightfully luxurious morning dream state. Yesterday was the work-horse, today is for relaxation and enjoyment.

No breakfast. One less thing to pack. Now my mornings are filled with sparkling clarity—light on my feet with senses alert. The world around me is much more vivid—with eyesight keen and hearing sharp. With nothing to cloud my brain, I'm locked precisely in the moment.

Nature's silent message rings loud and clear.

Nature's message can only be heard in wilderness silence. She speaks a silent truth beyond words and thought—transcending names, labels, science. The message is simple and pure, but when you try to define it, it vanishes into thin air. And in that vanishing, you find it again. Like a beautiful butterfly that can never be caught. Try and catch her and she'll drive you mad, eluding you for all of eternity. But learn to fly with her, and all the wonders of the world will be shown, and all the answers to your questions be known.

The very meaning of life is held in this delicate silence. Animals live in this silence all the time, as do the trees, the rocks, the sun. Even the soil *breathes* this silence. It's us who bring our noisy minds into nature, full of details, anxiety, and mindless chatter. We carry the noise and clamor of the city. But if we learn to quiet our minds and listen along with these silent beings, nature's message can finally be heard.

The animals are saying...

Stop, breathe, look around. Life is beautiful and full of boundless love. Now go, run, play— celebrate the day.

And the trees say...

This clean air, this pure water, these sparkling mountains; the sun, the moon, the stars and the planets—

*do you not see? They are all here for you. You are in
heaven. You've been here all along.*

And the rocks say...
*There is nowhere to go, nowhere to hide. Stop run-
ning—you have arrived.*

A squirrel twitches, gives a curious glance, as if to say...
*Does this one get it? I think this one gets... No. Could
it be?*

In all that silence, just for a moment, we do get it.
We've stopped thinking long enough to tap into the silent
wisdom of nature. For just a fleeting moment—

We are sane.

Like the trees who stand, day after day, year after
year, century after century, witness to all. Soaking up
life through their roots, inhaling through their leaves and
exhaling so that we too can breathe. Trees are shining
examples of being here now. With nowhere to go, no wars
to fight, no obligations, no deadlines to succumb to, each
is a unique window unto the world, relinquishing truth
to whoever wishes to listen. Silent beings of awareness,
energy, and light. Messengers of peace, reason, and sanity. In a world slowly going insane.

Like the rocks who witness, through the eons of time, poised stately against the deep blue sky. Mighty watchmen presiding over the land. Lifeless? Hardly. Rocks harbor the very wisdom of the core of Earth. Emanating truth like an orchestra, a symphony, a resounding wall of silence. They are the very foundation on which we stand. To them we owe it all. If there is anything worth worshipping, it is the rocks.

Like the sun who beams, down upon us from above, that fiery ball of energy at the center of the universe, precisely aligned so that we may exist. Any closer and we would burn, any further and we would freeze. If there is truly a god it is the sun, hanging in this delicate, perfect balance, shining her light, giving us life. Reminding us each day that we are the lucky ones. To be born on Earth is to be born in paradise itself.

The sun says...

Do you see how lucky you are? Every day I shine my light so that you may live. Go now and celebrate the day. Play beneath my shining rays, and shine your own light I give you every day. Spread the miraculous love and beauty that is the Earth. You are the reason that I shine. Please don't box yourself in. Set yourself free, this is your time to play in the forests, sing with the birds, frolic in the streams,

swim in the oceans. Sing, dance, shine like I do every
day, without judgment, fear, hatred, or greed. Earth is
the most abundant of all planets, and there is plenty to
go around.

And so it goes on...

Stay in the forest long enough and you'll begin to hear
the sermon. As much as we've taken from Mother Earth,
her love is still stronger than ever; it will never die. Earth
wants nothing but our gratitude—to celebrate our good
fortune to be Earthlings—an honor greater than any
other. I do not take that title lightly. I don't know why I
get to live here, I just know that I'm one of the lucky ones,
as are all of you. For that I vow to never take for granted
this life, and to celebrate my existence every day. There
is no reason whatsoever that we are here. No goal that we
must accomplish. No great task that we must fulfill. We
are simply here to live and that is that.

We create our own world—what a wonderful world!—
complete with pizza joints and ice cream parlors, super-
markets and fluorescent McDonalds. We've created
incredible art and music, fine restaurants and concert
halls, trains, planes, and automobiles that take us anywhere we wish to go. There are farms to grow food for
the masses, factories to produce gadgets of all variety,

and an infinite number of books to read, movies to watch, albums to listen to, games to play.

What's important to remember
Is that it is, in fact, a game.

Entertainment, amusement. We could sustain ourselves on nuts and berries alone. We *choose* our civilized world, myself included, and there is absolutely nothing wrong with that. But if we forget that we're playing the game, we run the risk of entertaining ourselves to death. Are we nearing that point? We have every luxury, every gadget, every imaginable form of entertainment at our fingertips, yet depression is at an all-time high. We live at the safest time in history, yet suicide rates are peaking. We are well-fed, with more people suffering from obesity than starvation. We've reached a point in history when we're more likely to overeat than to starve, more likely to kill ourselves than be killed.

If this is not a sign,
I don't know what is.

Here we are—safe and well-fed, with a roof over our heads and every sort of gadget at our fingertips. What on earth are we worrying about so much? We've all but guaranteed our survival. What is all this running around, this anxiety, this depression, this uneasiness? Running faster and faster, working harder and harder, so that someday we might have happiness in our lives? If there was ever a time to be happy, it is now. We have it all. There is nothing left to do but celebrate our victory. We have won the game!

Or have we?

Without wilderness, we are doomed to become lost inside our own devices, entertaining ourselves to extinction. *The species that amused itself to death.*

But wait...

Enlightenment is just around the corner, beyond the city lights, the smog, the noise, the traffic. It's just down the road, down a forest trail, in a sparkling meadow where the water still flows free, the air is still clear, the stars still visible in the night sky. Therein lies the truth of why we are here, and how we must continue. If we tame the last wild places, our truth will be lost, leaving us trapped inside our own game of winners and losers, competition and greed—trampling one another in our own imagined race to the top, all so that we can finally win the game of happiness. But there is no game to be won, no happiness to be found, no reward for all our needless suffering in our imaginary future. Just a dead end. An illusion, a big prank we've played on ourselves to keep us from enjoying the only thing in life that actually exists: the great and powerful, joyful and stupendous, thrilling and sensational, never-ending now!

Upon such revelation—things change.

We start asking questions like: "Am I climbing the ladder of success because it's fun, or simply because it's the next rung?" If it's fun then by all means... we keep climbing. But if we're miserable we begin to question our motives.

One consideration is raising a family. Because we are sacrificing, we may feel our suffering is justified. While noble by intent, this theory contains a major flaw. Children learn by example. If we are not enjoying life, neither will they, thus continuing the cycle of doing work that makes us miserable, just to raise children do the same. To raise happy children, we must be happy ourselves. Why else procreate?

The cirque is alive with curious plants and flowers. The western giant hyssop, for example, grows in lavender clusters, looking like tiny cities of pagodas. The wild bergamot has aromatic leaves, used to make mint tea. The most intriguing is perhaps the western pasqueflower, with a bloom that resembles the hair of troll dolls. Some have freshly styled golden locks, while others look as if they've been through a tornado, letting their freak flags fly wildly in the wind.

Springs flow up from the ground, requiring no filtration. When I'm thirsty, I simply dip my bottle for a drink, the water icy cold and refreshing. A warm breeze is constant, and there are no mosquitos in sight. Why, you ask, do mosquitos exist? So that we might cultivate new appreciation for the breeze. I celebrate by getting naked, washing the dirt, sweat, and sunscreen off my body, then drying in the warm sunshine. With the proliferation of bugs, being naked in the wilderness is a luxury I've not been able to indulge on this trip. Now it feels extravagant, the wind caressing my bare skin, my freshly washed feet and toes. Oh, to be clean again! Baptized in holy mountain water. A richness fit for a king, yet here I am—penniless—with every luxury at my fingertips.

I stay in the cirque for hours. Observing, writing, relishing this decadent day of relaxation and celebration. Never have I felt so clear, so open, with hour after hour of ecstatic awareness, mindfulness, openness. How magnificent the mind when free from incessant thought— open to all that surrounds! I cannot bring myself to leave, as I'd only be substituting one paradise for the next

—*backpacker's dilemma.* So I continue basking in the glory of eternal holiness.

When I finally break camp and head up the trail toward Horton Pass, the views open up further. Higher I climb into the clouds, through this land of enchantment. Water gushes down the mountain with full velocity, the snow melting faster now in the heat of the sun. There are acres of granite, with large terraces for camping at every turn. A true backpacker's paradise. I want to stop and stay at them all, but then there are the lakes—the lakes! Feeling pulled in every direction, I keep walking, toward the lake basin. The lofty terraces will just have to wait.

When I reach the pass I hit snow. It seems I could not have planned this trip any earlier. I slosh through the wet snowfields. I've packed no ice ax so I dig my heels firmly into the snow with each step, ensuring I don't slip and take an unexpected ride. There are fresh bear prints molded into the soft snow, subtly reminding me of their hidden presence. I make it safely through and begin my descent, toward the lake basin below.

The east fork of the Lostine River comes into view, winding its way through lush grass with snakelike curves. Upper Lake emerges, then Mirror Lake with all of its perches and outcroppings. The lakes will likely be crowded so I make camp high in the rocks. Then I head the rest of the way down, cross the Lostine, and hike on toward Mirror Lake.

As suspected, the lakes are bustling with campers. People always flock to the lakes. There is something about water that humans simply cannot resist. Mirror is gorgeous and a peaceful stroll ensues through this small forest community. Colorful tents dot the shoreline, each one in view of the next, but no one seems to care. There are mostly families in large groups, social campers enjoying all the joys that lake camping provides: swimming, fishing, tossing rocks into the water, gazing across Mirror's glassy surface, with Eagle Cap Mountain dominating the view.

I talk to several campers along the way. Everyone is happy and enjoying themselves, despite the clouds of mosquitos hovering by the water. After several days of silence, it's strange to hear my own voice. It's not often we get a break from people, let alone ourselves. After bustling Upper and Mirror, I make my way down to a group of smaller lakes to find some privacy for a swim. On a secluded beach sheltered by rocks, I strip out of my clothes and jump in, splashing around in a private lagoon. Then I stroll back to my solitary camp in the bluffs. Being around other people was a good way to acclimate to tomorrow's return to civilization, but one more night of solitude I can't resist. Social life will be here soon enough.

Dusk.

The weekend is approaching and more and more campers flood the basin, scrounging the highlands for places to camp as the sun begins to sink. I can't shake the urge to climb back to the lofty terraces near the pass and find a more solitary place to spend my last night. After dinner I pack my things and get back on the trail. Instantly I feel great, happy with my decision. In the cool evening air the climb is effortless. Dashing up the mountain at a borderline sprint, I leave the crowds behind, embracing the newfound solace of the upper highlands. In a mile I reach the plateau, just below the pass, where the granite stretches far and wide. I leave the trail, head out across the open rock, and pitch a new camp under the light of the crescent moon.

A true island in the sky. I look up and immediately see a shooting star. This will do, this shall be just fine. I try to follow my instincts, however irrational they seem. The move took less than forty-five minutes, now I have a private suite on top of the world. Why settle for anything less? The crisp air gave me fresh energy and I stay up late into the evening, gazing at stars, drinking tea, hunting for meteors. Under the Milky Way, I fall asleep to soft wind and exquisite alpine silence.

In the morning, orange sunshine greets me like an old friend. I open my eyes periodically, watching the sunrise until it peaks, then fall back asleep. When it gets too hot I climb out and prepare coffee under the shade of a dwarf pine. My last dose of morning stillness. The coffee mixes well, as it always does, and eases me into a more-than-perfect final morning in the "land of winding water." Today I'll reunite with Valerie and resume our great voyage of the Pacific Northwest. How I long to see her beautiful face.

CHAPTER TEN

Holy Cross Wilderness, Colorado

I HAD TO GET OUT—one last time before the snow, while the mountains are still golden, brisk, empty. I drive westbound on I-70, under Colorado bluebird skies with no traffic, on a road I've driven a hundred times before. In two hours I pull off the highway, onto a two-lane road that soon changes to gravel, then to dirt. Each change in the road surface changes me—shifting my internal gears from high to low. My breathing slows, my heartbeat steadies, and my old Toyota grinds up the rocks, through creeks, marshy meadows, until road's end at Fall Creek.

I park, step out of the truck, and shoulder my pack at once. My trip is short—so everything is packed.

All I must do now is walk. The simplicity of my departure adds to the overall sense of peace and calm as I effortlessly transfer from one world to the next. Enveloped by deep woods, I hike up the musty trail, damp with aspen leaves and pine needles, squeezing between boulders draped in tapestries of moss and ferns—hallways to different rooms, doors to new dimensions. My pack is light and I'm hindered by no fatigue as I rise toward the alpine expanse above the trees.

Streams are flowing nicely for this time of year, last year's winter bounty still brimming with sweet jubilation. Wildflowers abound, grass and shrubs are lush and verdant, and soon my doorway opens, bringing forth massive views of the Sawatch Range. Holy Cross Wilderness embodies the quintessential beauty of the Rockies, with waterfalls erupting from shimmering granite, cascading through luscious wildflower gardens, before joining Fall Creek beside the trail where I now walk.

Colorado you are part of me now.
Your blood runs through my veins.

The canopy thins as I start to enter that magical world above the trees where everything glows in ethereal light. The city of dreams. I'm flooded by emotion as sparkling meadows roll out like red carpet, studded with jeweled lakes and sparkling silver streams. The sounds of water fill the basin as I stroll with my head in the clouds and my feet planted firmly on the ground. Rather than whimsical, I'm clear-minded, with senses on full throttle, blood surging with oxygen, serotonin releasing into every cell. High on glory, bathed by the light of God.

Our vocabulary is far too primitive to reasonably describe such transformation. How it can happen so fast simply evades me—the experience not diminished by repeated outings, but rather intensified each time. Instead of building up a tolerance to such ecstasy, I seem to continue where I left off last time, increasing sensitivity and awareness with each outing. The experience is no altered state, but rather ultimate reality. No longer limited to my narrow field of focus, I'm open to all points of view, experiencing everything new for the first time without my human filter altering what lies ahead. My mind explodes with amazement at every little thing I encounter.

Filters are necessary at times. Without them it would be undoubtedly difficult to get things done. But this is precisely why we need wild places. We must have sacred spaces to safely remove our filters and see what's behind, remembering they are only tools. We must experience the sacredness, serenity, incomparable beauty, and unconditional love that resides beyond our narrow field of focus. Not forever—but for now!

We need holy lands, fountains of youth, gateways to something greater than ourselves. Glimpses into the boundless, infinite universe in which we reside.

Heaven is here—*up here!*—waiting to be experienced firsthand. Through the pearly gates I walk under shining cathedrals of light, into the wondrous lands of the Holy Cross.

I stroll across open tundra until I find a solitary retreat in the heavens. Then I get right to pitching camp so that everything is ready and there are no distractions to sitting in wonder. I open a notebook to record the moment, but rather than interrupt the experience with thinking, I start scribbling fanatically—my writing hardly legible even to myself, because if I slow down long enough to think, I may lose grasp. So I allow the writing to flow freely, unedited, unrestrained.

Rocks inhale, trees exhale, and waterfalls sing in great crescendos, echoing off the walls of a great fortress. Fall is here and the sun's rays blaze orange rather than yellow—their angles low, dramatic—casting long shadows across the land. The air invokes a chill as dense as the wintry clouds passing overhead, forcing me into all my layers. But this is all fine and welcome because the mosquito clouds have all but vanished. I am free to relax without the constant swatting of the little pests.

I fix dinner and it starts to rain. Temperatures plummet quickly, inviting early slumber and a night of long luxurious dreams.

I can only point a finger toward the wilderness experience; you must go yourself to understand. I can only show you the map and say—*there!*—above our cities, traffic jams, and smog exists the Holy Cross. Go find it, then come back and tell the others, so they too will know that wilderness is sacred—that it's worth saving beyond everything else. Profits can wait. Materials can wait. Desires can wait. To strip bare the holiest of nature's cathedrals is to deface the house of God itself.

There is no greater cause
Than the preservation of wilderness.
Our very survival depends on it.

The Earth is trying to teach us to live better. To lead richer, happier lives. To reside in harmony with the rest of nature. Nature's silent message suggests the existing of something far greater than what we see on the surface. It's about breaking through old patterns so that new ones may emerge. Wilderness will help if we only listen.

Morning.
Wind. Cold. Freezing rain. Winter is on its way yet still the sun emits bursts of light, piercing holes in the clouds, racing past the peaks, turning the frozen mist to glitter.

Despite the cold, the morning is full of magic. We are in limbo, hanging between seasons by a thread. Snow will be here soon. I can see patches lingering in the peaks, remnants of last year's storms. I pray for another big season, covering the mountains in blankets of powdery fluff. But please, can I have just one more sunny day?

Backpacking teaches us about *being*—as opposed to doing. With everything on your back, you can stop anywhere for the night and eat anytime you wish. Beyond that, there's nothing much to worry about. If it rains you put on rain gear, if it's cold you put on another layer, if you're tired you rest. It's about the *entire experience*.

Doing is completely different from being. When we are *doing*, our focus is highly narrowed. There's always a goal, a task, a destination. Our brains love *doing*, and get right down to business. We race through life in a blur, focused on a tiny sliver of reality, a sort of altered state—a CliffsNotes version of the world. Perceiving life only in terms of how it can serve us, rather than for what it truly is.

While backpacking, focus can expand outward rather than inward, letting you witness everything at once—this is where the magic happens. Now you're on the wavelength of trees, rocks, soil. They know *being* quite well:

HOLY CROSS WILDERNESS. COLORADO | 119

they live it all the time. So out here, among them, we connect on a much deeper level. This is the trick to hearing the silent message.

CHAPTER ELEVEN

Music Canyon / The Great Abyss

UNDER A FOREST OF SAGUAROS we wake to the sound of music. Birds are singing, butterflies dancing, all to the glory of the Superstition Mountains.

This canyon—a verdant desert where sand does not blow—is anchored by grasses, shrubs, and blooming gardens of cacti. Prickly pear, fishhook, agave, jumping cholla. The barrel, the beehive, the rainbow, the hedgehog. And the greatest, stateliest, mightiest of them all: the saguaro. With arms outstretched, angling toward the sun, these jolly giants celebrate spry character and zesty flamboyance. Some have many arms, dancing, waving, bending in all sorts of ridiculous ways, twisting and contorting in maddening configurations. Oddballs. Jokers in the deck. Others are single units, plain as cucumbers, true as telephone poles. Still others are elegant, dignified, with neither flaw nor blemish—two arms assume the proper position, like a Hollywood movie poster, a Vegas billboard, a flashing neon sign. So enigmatic and self-expressive, as they beam striking individuality unto the world.

Oh, to be a cactus! Functioning flawlessly in their unique and vivacious ways. In their presence, I feel not a traveler but a part of the story, a character in the play, a piece to the puzzle.

Further, deeper we plunge into a chorus of crickets, strange birds, and hidden owls. The delicate tinkling of water drifts in from the canyons, the desert brimming with abundance. Hopping from stone to stone, wading through pools with shoes and socks in hand, we splash through the afternoon, delighting in the warmth of springtime in the desert. Such is life in Music Canyon.

In the late afternoon, we arrive at Terrapin— a bizarre land of rust-colored spires, forks, fins and pinnacles—and a fine location for tonight's camp. Jagged formations erupt from hillsides of impossibly green flora. Gurgling creeks invoke tranquil content. Oh, the reluctance to leave, the urge to stay! But we are out of food, with just a handful of nuts and a full day's walk ahead—*backpacker's diet*. Must get in shape for those burgers and fries, pretzels and beer.

In summer, this place would be burnt to a crisp—every last drop of water sucked dry. Uninhabitable, inhospitable, unsurvivable. Every place has its season. Spring, summer, winter, or fall—migrate like the birds and have them all. Unfortunately, we've designed our lives to stay in one place, hence our restless nature.

But travel can be cheap, even cheaper than staying put. How much do we spend on our houses, expensive furnishings, late model cars—and the bills, insurances, and upkeep that comes with them? Not to mention the curse that follows:

The Fear—the fear of loss.

With all this stuff, we couldn't just uproot, we could lose *everything*. So we work to maintain an extravagance we cannot afford: mortgages, loans, credit cards. Robbing us of our freedom. Working to spend, spending to work. An unnerving cycle.

But to travel...

What do we need? A home base is nice—perhaps a small apartment or condo would do, or a van or RV. Less demanding travelers will argue you need no residence at all. I've tried both and found each a workable arrangement. Books like *Vagabonding* by Rolf Potts, and *How to Live in a Car, Van or RV* by Bob Wells, enlighten us with the information that a simplistic life of travel is far cheaper than we think. There's an incredible world out there, and some glorious wilderness left to explore.

It's the information age—it's taking over our lives. Technology is a fabulous tool. Without the internet I could not have published this book, nor created the blog that started this whole crazy business. But forget that it's a tool, and technology uses us. We become its slave, checking smartphones maniacally for each text, each ping, each notification. Give me something—anything! A scrap of hope to latch onto before that terrible dread creeps in. Our devices should come with warnings:

Contents highly addictive, may cause
shortened attention spans, and symptoms of
severe withdrawal.

Must we require constant stimulation each waking moment of our lives? Buzzing, grinding, scraping at our very souls? I mention this only because it happens to me.

Over and over it happens to me, until I can no longer take the madness. Fortunately there is a way out, an emergency escape, a backdoor exit. It's called wilderness.

Peace of mind is free for the taking. Not just the ones with deep pockets who stay in plush hotels, take the guided tour, follow the tourist route—all the while clinging to smartphones checking emails, stocks, bank accounts. The Fear follows—it will never leave, haunting your travels, sabotaging your dreams.

Money does not buy peace of mind.
Detachment from money buys peace of mind.

When we simplify our lives, we regain the freedom we once had as children, but with the wisdom of age. When we are young we have time but no money. When we are older we have money but no time. It's never too late to jump back in—back to the childlike essence of our youth. There is a way out of our materialistic ways. It just takes a little decluttering.

When our lives are filled with clutter, our belongings become lifeless objects with little meaning. When we simplify, we rekindle the magic of an old spoon, cookpot, coffee mug, sleeping bag. They become like old friends. Wood, cotton, leather, or steel—everything is alive, sacred and real—part of the Earth itself.

To children, the personalization of objects comes naturally. Rocks, stuffed animals, plastic toys and trucks—

they even give them names. It's only when we teach them what's real and what's not that they begin to second-guess their natural born instincts. Backpackers develop relationships with gear, craftsmen build relationships with trade tools, hunters form relationships with their guns and knives—just as Native Americans developed deep bonds with bows and spears, arrowheads and clay pots. It's when we treat our possessions like refuse that we disconnect from the sacredness of life: things we use once and forget, leading to the hordes of unloved junk that gets tossed out daily. If we chose our belongings like we chose our lovers, would landfills be so large? If instead of reckless purchasing we formed relationships with our gear, would Walmarts and Super-Targets even exist? When everything in our lives holds great meaning, peace of mind prevails.

The more we simplify, the freer we become. The freer we become, the less we cling. The less we cling, the closer we are to God. Until we finally reach the end of our days, standing at the precipice of life, staring out into the face of the unknown. Then we shall be ready to hurl ourselves into the great abyss—stripped bare of money, possessions, clothes, skin and bones. Free...free at last.

"Freedom's just another word for nothing left to lose."
–*Janis Joplin*

CHAPTER TWELVE

Sun Salutation

We hang in the balance.

The sun has begun her journey
To the other side of the Earth.
Slowly she slips behind the curtain,
Teasing us with fleeting warmth.

And we hang in the balance.

Soon everything will change.
Evening will be underway
As winter darkness looms.

But for a moment more,
It's summer.

And we hang in the balance.

I am the naked man,
Perched on cold stone,
Praying to the sun,
Basking in the light,
Soaking up the great power,
So that I might take some back with me
To the other side.

And we hang in the balance.

Soon I'll be climbing into long johns,
Winter hat, down jacket.
But for a moment more
My bare skin is warm to the touch,
A great receptor of heat and energy,
Every pore infused with the Divine.

I dare not move.
I've walked days to get to this rock,
This sunset, this moment.
All my life I've been wandering
To get *here*.

And we hang in the balance.

A rock falls from some distant cliff.
If I were directly beneath I would be crushed.
Guess it's not my time.
When it does come I think I'll be ready.

The rock smashes into the ground,
Explodes into a thousand pieces,
Races down the sandstone like marbles,
Each assuming new form, new shape, new purpose.

Far below they rest
As silence rushes in again
With new vengeance.

And we hang in the balance.

She dips her toe,
Testing the waters before taking the plunge.
Things are moving quickly now,
Faster and faster she drops,
Until just a sliver remains.

And we hang in the...

CHAPTER THIRTEEN

The Silent Message

I PARK MY TRUCK NEXT TO A DRAINAGE, guzzle the last of my coffee, and stumble down the sand into a ditch. The approach is non-dramatic, but I can see domes of sandstone in the distance, glowing golden with morning light, rolling off toward the horizon. The air is pleasingly warm this late in the fall, but there's a cold front moving in—another problem for another day. Right now it feels like summer.

In a mile the land drops out from beneath me, forming a narrow crack in the earth, looking like the aftermath of an earthquake. I lower myself and my pack down into the slot, accessing the cool chamber below. At the bottom I find a lovely stream filled with minnows.

I follow the watercourse, winding its way through the shadows, into the heart of the Utah desert.

Side canyons reveal themselves, each an invitation to the mystery. November skies cast deep shadows, dramatizing features with theatrical light. I walk several miles before finally heading up one of the tributaries. My choice is random, moving in one direction, then another, off toward some alluring rock formations above. I walk until I feel sufficiently isolated, immersing myself into the experience—for better or worse. The canyon constricts, stretches, yawns—at the end I find a large slickrock expanse. Home sweet home.

Morning.

That cold front came in, just like they said it would. Now it's freezing. The wind—that's the problem. When calm, the 30-degree air feels tolerable, but when it howls, the bitterness cuts through my bones like daggers. I forwent the tent last night, sleeping directly on the rock— pretty comfortable, until I could no longer take the sand blasting the left side of my face. A sinister, unnerving gale. I tried burrowing deeper into my bag, but it was no use. Sand always finds a way. So I got up, erected the tent in the middle of the night, in the middle of the windstorm, which was a disaster. But things got much better once inside the tent. I could finally sleep in peace.

I boil water in a small patch of sun, struggling to control the stove, trying to prevent my pot from blowing over. Sand in my coffee I can deal with; the main problem is my right eye—there seems to be a piece of sand that I cannot get out. Now there's this persistent scratchiness.

There are things we must cope with to get to the goods. I forget about the hard times, because the good ones are so damn good. I forget about the gritty teeth, sandblasted skin, burning eyes, frozen hands. But I keep coming back. It takes time, but the journey is worth it. I'll continue until I'm too old, or too lazy. Then I'll go live on an old houseboat, idling away my remaining days gazing out over the water, contemplating existence—going *inside* during frozen windstorms. Well, maybe.

Right now, this is where I choose to be. Thrashed. Sandblasted. Exposed. Scrapes on my knees, aches in my joints, stinky feet, sand in my eye. *In it*, like everything else. Yet the urge grows stronger to burrow deep, make a nest, hibernate.

I'm always out here at the edge of the seasons. The weather unstable and unpredictable. The desert can be harsh in any season. In summer there's the heat and flash floods. In winter you get snow and bitter temps. Spring and fall are best, but even then you don't know what'll be thrown at you. Wind, rain, sandstorms? Crystalline stillness? All is possible. Perhaps this is just Mother Nature's attempt to thrash me around a bit—wake me up, snap me out of it—before dishing out the goods.

To transcend,
We must walk through the fire.

Wind rages, the sun blasts, the desert quivers. Sand is the architect, scouring at porous stone, leaving domes, caves, arches. When I stare out, it all looks like chaos—no possible way of revealing a route—an endless sea of light and shadow. But over the years I've learned how to navigate these places, following the paths of water rather than footprints. Where water flows there is a way, perhaps not for a human, but a way nonetheless. They create maps on the ground. Follow them and you'll find magic. Or nothing. That's the allure. The unknowing. Places you can go freeze your ass off for a bit, or get lost, or die. Mother Nature will have her way, as she always does. Trust her and she'll show you her secrets. Spite her and she'll turn an indifferent hand—leave you to the vultures.

There is a method here. An ancient way of communication. I'd say secret, but it's no secret at all. The rest of nature understands it perfectly fine. We've forgotten how to subdue our thoughts and listen with feeling. The trees, the animals, the rocks, the sun and the moon, even the wind—they communicate in song. Improvisational music we can tap into anytime if we listen with our hearts and quiet our minds. This music invokes deep feeling inside all those who listen, transmitting wisdom without words.

True artists know the message well. Great musicians understand the place from which all music comes—when no one is playing it. That deep level of unspoken communication that occurs when the groove is just right, the mind relaxes, and pure feeling runs the show.

Nature is no different. Here the song is played indefinitely. The music never stops. If you open your heart, in exactly the way you listen to music, you may begin to hear the wisdom without words. This message is highly intelligent, and far beyond the capacity of our thinking minds. When truly grasped, our meager, rationalizing brains seem paltry—like we're children playing with toys, thinking our childish game is the real world. How insignificant we've become, no longer able to hear the music of life, too selfish to even listen.

We've deemed ourselves too important. Too busy to play in the dance of life. Nature has been reduced to a static backdrop for our all-consuming human activity, a pile of resources to be exploited and serve the needs of humanity alone. A nice place for a picnic—when we are finished doing more important things, if we have time. We've forgotten that everything in nature affects everything else. Every action has consequence: good, bad, or indifferent. It's all there in the message. If we care to listen.

This is no great epiphany. It's actually extraordinarily basic on every level. The most fundamental of all truths.

Every action creates an equal and opposite reaction—the rest of nature understands this without thinking. It's thinking that got us into this mess. Thinking that's made us mad. Our refusal to accept the most basic of truths is no less than psychotic. How else to describe it? It's time we relearned how to listen to the never-ending song of Earth. Only the truth shall set us free.

I hike down into a nest of boulders to get out of the wind. Now I have a bird's-eye view of the canyons, sheltered from the frigid breeze. What is it about the desert? That's the eternal question. There is less life here, much less than in the forests, which possess a childlike essence—youth, vitality, playfulness, curiosity. Deserts possess an older knowledge, vast and infinite. Place your hand upon an aging tree and feel wisdom. Sit upon these stone monoliths and feel all-knowingness, older than time. We'd be wise to listen to what they have to say. Experiencing gratitude is how to hear them best. There is something about this emotion that opens us up, tunes us into a different frequency.

Rocks speak through an audible vibration that commands respect, yet at the same time feels welcoming, embracing. Through the rocks, we are getting closer to the core of the Earth itself. When everything has been stripped away, the rocks remain. Exposed to the light, soaking up great power, eon after eon.

Wilderness silence allows nature's message to best be heard, but the mind must also be quiet. The best way to silence the mind is by experiencing awe. With so much openness and vastness, awe comes naturally in the desert—like a shock to the system—that something so immense can remain undeveloped, untouched, unspoiled—ineffably beautiful. The mind cannot process it—so it stalls, gasps, peters out. In awe, we become aware that there is something far greater than ourselves. And it's filled with beauty and glory and brilliance. And we can dance around the truth all we want, trying to reduce the world into words and symbols, scientific facts and charts, but when we get down to the essence of things, we cannot escape the undeniable truth:

Love is all there is.

Love. A four-letter word of our own invention, plastered inside every greeting card at Walgreens, yet perhaps closer to the truth than any other combination of letters, numbers, facts, figures, graphs, or charts used to describe the universe. Love—when truly felt—evokes something deep inside us that surpasses logic. Love, like awe, is pure feeling. And feeling is the essence of life.

When we experience love we are connected—part of the dance. When we love, we become the music again, and merge back into the song of life. Harmonizing with the rest of creation. We are born as love, we die as love, and if we are lucky, we live as love. Unless we are too busy trying to find it.

Morning.

I'm calling for an off day. There are plenty of places to roam right from camp, I see no need pack up and hike on. Everything I could want is here. My camp is south facing, allowing for maximum sun exposure. My front lawn extends for acres, out to terraces, bluffs, private nooks. There are shallow caves, rock houses, and large expanses of slickrock to roam about freely. There are areas I can hide from the wind if I choose, or lie down in the shade for a snooze. I can walk barefoot out over the polished rock, or amble down to the creek and enjoy a drink under the singing cottonwoods. There are wild, unnamed canyons. All of this—right outside my door.

The bushes still have their leaves, and some are starting to change color. There are yellow flowers everywhere, soaking up the last rays of autumn. The entire desert is adorned in the rich colors of fall, evoking feelings of thanksgiving, celebration, and general pleasantness.

The sky is exquisite, crisp and blue without a single cloud. The nearest airport is four hundred miles away. There are no machines in the sky, no chemtrails, no human-made sounds whatsoever. Just the delicate singing of the canyons themselves.

As the day warms, my world changes from harshness to decadence, easing me into the paradise I long for—my moment is arriving. The pains and discomforts of the last few days seem trivial to what's awakening now. The howling wind has diminished to nothing more than a sub-tle whisper, revealing hidden secrets from distant lands too mysterious to comprehend. If I cannot explore every mountain, every canyon, every spring—then perhaps they shall come to me in song. If I listen deeply enough. If I'm patient enough. If I just stay out here long enough.

A prolonged detachment from the familiar is required to achieve the unknown. The longer I remove myself from the workings of mankind, the better I'm able to hear the whispers in the wind, the voices in the cottonwoods, the murmurs in the streams. These sounds—they intertwine, wrapping around each other like serpents in a ritual dance, with a beauty that touches my soul intimately. Plucking the strings of my very own heart, vibrating inside my chest, causing me to weep. Filling me with boundless love.

Our human sense of separateness is unique. It must be unlearned to reconnect with the rest of nature. In wil-derness, our way of thinking is the exception, not the rule, so it's easier to let it fall away. The sooner we let go of what's false, the easier we can get down to what's real.

How much better to be connected! The feeling is always the same—like a welcome home. Like I've been away so long, asleep in a coma or false dream state. A caged bird set free.

The whispers cease and the desert grinds to a sudden halt, exposing a new layer of profound silence. I want desperately to grab ahold of it and not let go—to become part of what's inside—an all-encompassing energy of warmth and love and infinite wisdom. A doorway to heaven. A portal to God. A gateway to the soul.

But there is nothing to do with it. Nowhere to go. God is here—the source of all love and light. How easy to let in greatness when the mind has been sandblasted clean. The whole process seems so logical, so clear—traveling through darkness to experience the light.

What we want is to *feel*. That's why we're so drawn to music and art, movies and TV, drugs and alcohol, games and social media. Nature is *pure* feeling. This is evident when we step out into the wilderness and become overwhelmed by feelings without words. Words are maps—they point to the real thing, but are no substitute. When you get to the wilderness, it's time to put away the map. You've already arrived.

Evening comes quickly, as it will in November. Chased by shadows, I'm forced higher and higher up the canyon walls, stalking the last rays of the sun. Each ledge affords new vantage, exposing previously hidden passages, labyrinths, chambers. The land looks comforting and inviting. Shadows create new dimension, features I could not see in broad daylight: caves, slots, narrows, shimmering cottonwoods revealing the pathways of water, filling the canyons with glittering gleam. Some of the trees are changing into their fall attire, but most still shimmer like party beads in a St. Patrick's Day parade.

Beyond the cliffs I can see Glen Canyon, where the Colorado River flows into Lake Powell, a hidden network of underwater canyons, lost ruins, hidden springs. To get there you'd need fins, oxygen tanks, underwater masks. Or for a few grand, a houseboat stocked with coolers of beer and ice, the scents of burgers and brats sizzling on the grill.

The last of the sun's rays peek over the canyon wall, showering me in a final blast of warmth, before leaving me for the long dark night.

Long dark night.

When the sun finally breaks, I climb from my tent and head to the place I call "the nook." The nook is a divot in the sandstone, precariously shielded from the wind, with open views facing south. I found this place yesterday and spent the entire evening there. My desert abode has many rooms, many features. Stretching out for at least a hundred yards to all sides, it's one of the finest camps I've stumbled upon. I'll likely return to this very canyon, as its beauty and accessibility are unparalleled. With year-round running water, I can visit in any season. There are no washed-out or muddy access roads to contend with, and I haven't seen another human since I left the truck. Even if there were other campers, it would still be extremely easy to find solitude, as all you must do is stroll up any number of side canyons to find more springs, more benches, more nooks—or even access the rims up above. I'd call it paradise by all measures.

Today I'll explore further down canyon, possibly making it all the way to Lake Powell. Then it's another night on the terrace, under the cold moon, the shimmering stars. Three nights in one camp—a rarity, as my wanderlust is usually far too strong to stay any place more than one night. Always longing for distant vistas, somewhere new, even more magical than the last. But this resort of a campsite leaves little to be desired, with endless exploring from my doorstep, dizzying views, and more alcoves, benches, sundecks, and mezzanines than I could ever conceive.

The sky is happy—a lovely shade of blue with no cloud to be found. The breeze is steady and tolerable, especially in the nook. In fact, the micro-climate of the nook is extraordinary. I can see a stiff breeze blowing the plants and flowers below, yet all is quiet in the nook. The decadence envelops me and I find it difficult to move, explaining yesterday's full day of tea drinking. Is this camping or a week at the Hamptons? I feel like a king seated on a throne, with every desire at my fingertips, every whim easily satisfied with a simple reach to my right or to my left. This is full-tilt laziness, extreme lollygagging. Every day filled with pure possibility, yet with nothing particular that must be done.

When early hunters and gatherers returned from their long journeys, with food and supplies for their families, days of idleness must have ensued. I can feel my own good fortune deep inside my bones, blessed by the gods with richness and abundance. How lucky am I not to have to hunt, grow my own food, or make my own gear? How easy we have it—if we could only realize our own good fortune. We are rich as kings, wallowing in our wealth—continually grasping for more. What good are our riches if we cannot enjoy them fully, piling up our money so we can live when we're old—if we make it that far? When we're old it's too late, time to move on, make room for new birth. The time is now to take the money and run, out into the wild blue yonder, beyond our fenced-in, pay-as-you-go society, where the best things in life are free.

Another day on the terrace.

More tea, please.

The cliff dwellers must have had abundant free time to examine every nook, every cave, every terrace for sun factors, wind exposure, views and aesthetics. How the sun could heat up a rock wall, radiating warmth into the evening. How some areas could be howling on a windy day, while others remain peaceful and calm. How many others have used this canyon, this campsite, this very nook?

Utah's canyons are full of such luxuries, where you may feel cozy even when temperatures are freezing. The ancient people erected walls of rocks and mortar, providing extra protection from the elements, creating palaces in the sky that felt not just comfortable but decadent. When the sun began its slow journey north, their southern facing homes would become bathed in shadow, providing much-needed shade when temperatures climbed into the triple-digits. In the desert, any temperature may feel comfortable in the right place at the right time. They learned from the lizards and snakes, hiding under ledges in summer, lounging on warm rocks in winter.

The goal must have been comfort, safety, as well as aesthetics—with open views for security and surveillance. Why should we think they'd settle for anything less? Perhaps they felt they had found paradise. Sparkling canyons with year-round water and animals to hunt. When food was scarce they would tap into the sacred, dining on silence and intoxicating beauty. Trusting nature's cycles and rhythms.

No doubt, they could hear nature's silent message, basking in the sublime day after day. Tuned in to the Earth's frequency, they would know just when the time was right to hunt—waiting patiently until the moment arrived. With respect and gratitude, they would have been guided to all the right places, navigating by feel and intuition—like the rest of the desert.

There would have been little separation between themselves and the other animals. They painted depictions of humans morphing into birds, lizards, and bighorn sheep. To survive they must have learned from animal behavior; how they hunted, found water, sought shelter.

Canyons reveal an ancient way of being that is anything but linear. A way of living that's embodied in the rocks. A wisdom that the trees, plants, and animals have been feeding on for millennia. There's a way of moving down here that surpasses thought. You literally feel your way through, with instinct steering the ship.

Like navigating an ocean reef or wild river, landing a small plane. You learn by what feels right. Moving toward the *good* and away from the *bad*. To ignore this sixth sense is to invite disaster—any pilot or captain knows this. To go unconsciously is to tempt death, like walking blindly into traffic, too lost in thought to sense what's real.

Nature is no landscape through which we travel. We are an integral part. Our self-preservation instincts prove that nature wants us to survive, but if we become disconnected, no longer a functioning part of the organism, we may be mistaken for a disease, an unwanted parasite, an intruder, an alien. Like a liver that refuses to filter blood, an intestine that refuses to digest food—we will be rejected, terminated. Staying in tune with nature is not just a lifestyle choice, it's crucial to our health and well-being, and the health and well-being of the larger organism known as Earth.

When Mother Nature no longer senses us as her own, we shall be cast aside like unwanted orphans. How much lovelier to surrender to the flow? Welcoming nature's message with open hearts. Embracing our mother, basking in the love we were meant to live in all the time.

We cannot save the Earth.
The Earth does not need saving.
We can only save ourselves.

The day is dawning that we must make a choice. Will we go down the path of the mechanical, maniacal mind? Lost in the endless cycles of our brains, drifting further and further into delusion, and the denial of our own natural state? Or will we open our hearts and reconnect, tuning into nature's frequency so that we may hear her wisdom loud and clear? Anyone with the capacity to think can project forward twenty, fifty, a hundred years, and see that we cannot continue along the path we are on. Something must change. Will we become lost inside our own game? Or will we step outside the boundaries of our thinking minds, gain new perspective, and see the larger picture?

This planet loves us. How can she not? We are her babies—and babies we are in relation to the rocks, the trees, the other animals. We are the new kids on the block. Will we evolve to become functioning members of society? Or will we remain as outcasts, transients, thugs, bastard children? Elitists who care only about themselves rather than that of the greater good? Gobbling up resources, killing in the name of false gods separate from the rest of nature. Another one of Earth's experiments gone south, like so many others before our time.

We are at war with ourselves.

There are two sides: The Heart versus The Mind.

This has nothing to do with politics, borders, race, religion, or economic class. Feeling has been shoved under the carpet for too long. The Heart of Humanity is opening. Will you join the revolution? All that's required is that you open your heart and relax your mind, tune back in to the frequency of the Earth, and become curious again—just as you did when you were a small child entering the world for the first time. You do not have to die to be reborn and see the world with fresh eyes.

We are born as pure love. Then we get too smart for our own good. Educated by our elders that feelings aren't to be trusted, that happiness lies in the future, that we are separate from what surrounds us. We stop seeing the rocks, trees, bugs, and other animals as our friends. Further and further we drift from our true identities— and nature, further and further into the background— until we no longer notice it. Then on occasion, when we experience a glimpse of rare unspoiled beauty, we wallow up, remembering for a split-second how beautiful and magical it all was—before we had to grow up.

Step back into that childlike essence. It can be effortless, natural, wonderful! If enough of us do this, it will become contagious. Just as unconsciousness is contagious, so is awareness. A shift will happen of its own accord if people begin to *feel* again. Mother Nature will embrace us, welcoming us home like lost children, and show us the way. There's a way out of all this thinking, and a way into knowing, if we just shut up and listen. There is nothing to be figured out if we tune into ultimate intelligence. The same intelligence that allows our blood to flow through our veins, bees to pollinate flowers, birds to fly south, salmon to spawn, whales to migrate, caterpillars to become butterflies, the Earth to rotate, the moon to orbit, and the rest of life to function perfectly of its own accord. All of it happens without thinking. We have access to this vast intelligence—if we just take the time to listen. The message is not difficult to hear when we open ourselves to feeling, exactly as the rest of nature does.

Enlightenment is just around the corner.
Wilderness is where it lives.

Morning.

The sun came earlier today, or so it seemed. The winds have retreated, leaving nothing but a subtle breeze. It's getting warmer every day. The cold front is dissolving, and we're settling into that sweet spot where life is easy. But as usual—like always—my food stores are running out. Soon I'll have to return to the truck to resupply.

This canyon has been more than good to me and I'll forever be grateful. I should like to return to this spot each year, as a sort of homecoming, a ritual, a tradition. To honor its imparted wisdom, and resume our cosmic conversation. Of all the canyons I've explored, this may be the friendliest and most solitary—a rare combination. If five-star accommodations are what you're looking for, this is the place, but I will not disclose its location. Some things you must discover for yourself. Fortunately, Utah is full of such marvels. There are literally thousands of lonely canyons, just like this, waiting to be explored. Many just off the highway. Get yourself a good map and look for the places with no signs, no routes, no trailheads—nothing but a dusty old wash on the side of the road. This is where you'll find your solitary bliss. Maybe. Or it'll fizzle out in a quarter mile. But always remember, this is entirely the point. In wilderness you get to be a kid again, an explorer of new routes, a discoverer of hidden treasures. In time, your maps will be riddled with highlighter marks and earmarked pages—your own library of gems and secrets. You needn't require a travel agent or a large retirement fund to travel, just a pioneering spirit.

On the day you were born, you inherited 640 million acres of the most stunningly beautiful landscape on Earth. We are beyond lucky to live in America. Free to safely explore land of our ownership.

If these places didn't exist, something essential would be lost. I'll never take for granted the privilege to walk, one foot in front of the other, in the direction of my own choosing. The opportunity to get lost so that I might find myself again. Each time I'm surprised at what I find.

Wilderness is my church, my teacher, my mentor, my psychologist, my mother, my savior. The school of life—where we learn not from books, nor words, nor lectures. A classroom where we learn not from that which thinks—but that which knows. The lesson is Truth itself. I can no more explain this than I can explain the sparkle in a baby's eyes, or falling in love for the first time, or the agony of heartbreak, the loss of a child, the death of a dream. Good, bad, or ugly—truth is undeniable. It cannot be run from, nor grasped by the mind, only experienced by the soul. Truth is what we come out here to find. It's why we trudge through sandstorms, freezing rain, and howling wind; walking on blistered heels with callused fingers and sunburned lips. Why we endure the long dark night.

Why would one leave the comforts of home,
To wander off into the wilderness alone?

I have no answers—only the direction in which to point. Cities are manifestations of our minds. We cannot escape the mind in a mind-dominated world. We must go to the wilderness to free ourselves from these confines and bring feeling back into our world. Look around—it's happening already. Architecture is becoming less rigid and more organic. In cities like Denver and Seattle, wild organic imagery is being painted on the sides of buildings and in alleyways. Noisy highways are being ripped down and placed underground, with parks and trees planted in their place. To the casual observer this is nothing more than aesthetics, but what's really happening is the embrace of feeling back into our communities. And the more we feel the more we connect—with each other and with nature. It takes time, but the journey is worth it.

Nature is feeling. Art invokes feeling, so the more we bring art into our lives, our cities, the more we welcome nature back into our beings. Art mimics nature. So with art we bring the natural world back into our stale, mind-dominated society. If we can't bring the masses into the wilderness—would we want to?—why not bring nature to the masses? The effect on the heart and mind is substantial, and helps tune us back into nature's silent message.

Transformation is not that difficult, and can happen in a relatively short period of time. Who would have thought that in a few short years we'd shift from The War on Drugs to legal marijuana? Now *60 Minutes* is doing episodes on the health benefits of psychedelic drugs, and CBD is being put in practically everything. Fear is being replaced with curiosity. Feeling receptors are opening up.

Burning Man, ayahuasca ceremonies, music and yoga festivals—they are attracting the masses. Humanity is sensing that there's something very essential we are missing out on. And it's been here all along. Society is slowly beginning to *feel* again. Like lost children, we are wandering home—finally coming to the realization that love is all we need.

Why we come out here defies logic—surpasses logic. Beyond the walls of civilization lies something profoundly more human than anything in our civilized world. When we go to the wilderness we discover our truest selves. We get to die for a moment, experience our Shangri-La, and become reborn with new eyes with which to view the world.

I stay another night. What changes my mind is a group of sandstone buttes to the east. From the main canyon I can see a possible route to the top, and they look lovely glowing in the warm afternoon sun. I *am* out of food, but beginning to believe I could dine on the silence and intoxicating beauty alone.

I leave the main canyon and climb a gully, which leads me to the base of the sandstone buttes—just as I'd hoped. Now for the fun part. There is something about walking on solid sandstone that's remarkably pleasing. The way rubber boot soles grip like Velcro, the way the rock is so clean and so smooth. There are two places you can comfortably camp barefoot. One is the beach, the other is slickrock. Both are made of sand, but sandstone is petrified, like a beach polished smooth.

When I reach the buttes I'm delighted to see that they go on and on, with lovely benches between them for camping. Looking down, I can see where I've been traveling for days, as well as several side canyons I'd not noticed. There is so much to explore I'm baffled, seeing now that I could return and never hike the same canyon twice.

I pitch my camp high in the buttes, surrounded by sandstone that rolls out for miles, off toward some snowy peaks in the distance. When the sun sets I make tea and lie down on the smooth rock, arms outstretched, staring up into the big blue sky. When the moon rises I go barefoot walking, off into the slickrock dreamscape.

Morning.

Winter has returned. Life has retreated and closed up tightly. One might say *dead*, but the spark of life lies hidden beneath—dormant—ready to resurge when warm weather returns. The chatter of desert life has all but ceased, leaving nothing but the rocks—for they never sleep, never hibernate, never cease their soundless roar. The band has left the stage, leaving only the rocks to perform their winter solo. In spring the full band shall reconvene, reuniting in grand concerto, celebrating their joyous return. The desert will once again be wild with song. But for now it's just the rocks humming together in great hymn. I'm the lone observer, audience of one, standing front and center for the greatest show on Earth. The price of admission was nothing but enduring the long dark night. Now I'm first in line for the rising of the sun, the thawing of the canyons, the cold hills, the frozen sand, my shivering bones.

The rocks will swallow you up in their vastness, take you into their world—show you things. Hold on tightly and you'll learn everything there is to know. Just don't try to make sense of it, or it shall crumble, and the rocks will become just rocks, and you will become just flesh and bone, and life will return to the stale world of words, descriptions, definitions.

The rocks are our wisest elders. When we tear them down we lose irreplaceable wisdom, slaughtering the last of our high priests, demolishing the last of our holy temples.

Desert dwellers were called to these rocks, making homes in the cliffs, decorating walls with fine art and imagery, soaking up the great power. The more they listened, the more they understood the inner workings of life, death, and rebirth. Transcending their own flesh and bone, taking up residence in the rocks themselves. They were shown wondrous things. Drawings depict aliens and otherworldly beings. Without the use of words, they carved and painted what they saw. Passing on to others that there is great magic to be found, if we just listen to the rocks—surrender to their monstrous energy.

Basking in ecstasy day after day, year after year, they absorbed great wisdom. What could that do to a person? To what great depths could they have traveled? Is there a limit to transcendence? When you become the great knower, what then?

CHAPTER FOURTEEN

Time Travel

HUMANS ARE BORN WITH AN EXTRAORDINARY GIFT: the ability to travel in our minds. Our incredible imaginations allow us to create vivid fantasies about the past and future. We've become so good at this, that we believe these fantasies to be real. Many have gone so far as to live in this state all the time. While such a condition might otherwise be considered delusional, this has become reality for millions of people. Many would even consider it normal.

It is anything but.

While past and future projection are useful tools, if left unattended they can cause entire civilizations to lose grasp on reality. The side effects of which are severe, including depression, drug and alcohol addiction, even suicide. When the affected individual finally gets relief from this terrible affliction, they feel an immediate high. The reason being, when delusional for such long periods of time, relief, even when brief, feels dramatic. Like experiencing sudden liberation from chronic pain, or waking up from a bad dream. This sense of high is no altered state, but rather our normal, natural state of being. Yet because we've suffered for so long, this "normal" state feels like a distant dream. Something we lost when our endless summers of childhood came to an end.

This condition, as far as we know, is unique to humans. Though other animals appear to learn from their mistakes, and make practical preparations for the future, they do not seem to make a problem of it.

If we want to heal the Earth, we must first heal ourselves. There is no other way out of this mess. Until we can see what is directly in front of our eyes, all efforts will be futile. We can learn from nature. The animals, the plants, the trees and the rocks, the moon and the stars— they will help us if we befriend them. But if we continue to study them as objects—something to be probed, dissected, examined—something outside of ourselves—we will continue down the same path as we have. If we make them our friends, embracing our shared existence, they will share their secrets and show us the way. Nature can help us wake up and return to our natural state. She is our best teacher, if we revere her as such. If we go on as we have, seeing her as a backdrop, a heap of resources, or something to be tamed and conquered—we will learn nothing.

The way out of delusion is through connection—with a tree, a flower, a bird, a rock. When we learn to see nature as our own kin, we will wake from this long strange dream. And the world will become alive again.

Enjoy this Book?
Write a Review!

If you've enjoyed my book, the best compliment you can give is writing a review. As a self-published indie author, I don't have the advertising power of a major publishing firm. But you can make a big difference.

Honest reviews help other readers find me. It only takes five minutes and the review can be as short as you like.

If you'd like to leave a review on Amazon.com, search for my title, click on *Customer reviews*, then click *Write a customer review*. Simple as that.

Thank you very much.

Dirt-Worshipping
Tree-Huggers Unite!

If you are interested in solo backpacking, or following along on my upcoming adventures via my blog, I'd love to connect with you!

Sign up for my mailing list and you'll gain access to:

- My ongoing travel essays.
- Exclusive photographs of wilderness areas from this book.
- Backpacking recipes, gear checklists, tips for finding your own gateway to the soul, and more.

You can sign up for my mailing list at
www.scottstillmanblog.com.

SAVE WILD UTAH!

SOUTHERN UTAH WILDERNESS ALLIANCE (SUWA)

SUWA is the only non-partisan, non-profit organization working full time to defend Utah's Redrock Wilderness from oil and gas development, unnecessary road construction, rampant off-road vehicle use, and other threats to Utah's wilderness-quality lands. Their power comes from people like you from across the nation who want to protect this irreplaceable heritage for all Americans.

If you'd like to get involved, please find them at **www.suwa.org**.

SOUTHERN UTAH WILDERNESS ALLIANCE

About the Author

Scott Stillman is bestselling author of the book, *Wilderness, The Gateway to the Soul.*

He was born in Fairfield, Ohio, then moved to Boulder, Colorado in 2003. Backpacking extensively through the mountains and deserts of the American West, he records his journeys with pen and notebook, writing primarily about our spiritual connection to nature. To stay on the wilderness path, he and his wife, Valerie, have lived in a camper and worked a slew of conventional and unconventional jobs to fund their travels.

You can find his blog and online home at:
scottstillmanblog.com
facebook.com/scottstillmanblog

If the mood strikes, send him an email at:
scottstillmanauthor@gmail.com

Made in the USA
Middletown, DE
10 September 2020